THE POCKET HUNTING & FISHING GUIDE

TIPS, TACTICS, AND MUST-HAVE GEAR

FOREWORD BY JAY CASSELL

SKYHORSE PUBLISHING

Skyhorse Publishing books may be purchased in bulk at special discounts for sales promotion, corporate gifts, fund-raising, or educational purposes. Special editions can also be created to specifications. For details, contact the Special Sales Department, Skyhorse Publishing, 307 West 36th Street, 11th Floor, New York, NY 10018 or info@skyhorsepublishing.com.

Skyhorse® and Skyhorse Publishing® are registered trademarks of Skyhorse Publishing, Inc.®, a Delaware corporation.

Visit our website at www.skyhorsepublishing.com.

10 9 8 7 6 5 4 3 2

Library of Congress Cataloging-in-Publication Data is available on file.

ISBN: 978-1-62914-185-5
Printed in China

Foreword

Every so often, you come across an old book that just gets it right, that still holds up years after it was published. Such is the case of the *Handy Book of Sportsmen's Secrets*.

First published in 1944, *Sportsmen's Secrets* came out in a year when World War II was still raging on, when the war effort pre-empted resources that might have been devoted to the development of new hunting and fishing gear. It was a time sportsmen had to rely on their skills more than ever, when ingenuity and woods skills made the difference between success and failure. *Sportsmen's Secrets* was the right book at the right time, a fact-filled gem that presents "interesting and novel methods of procedure—little-known methods which, although soundly founded on fundamentals, have new twists, fresh angles and approaches, novel short cuts, and stream-line efficiencies," to quote the original foreword. In a nutshell, the book is full of tips, tactics, and techniques, many of them novel at the time, but which have now stood the test of time and still apply today. Among some of the "new" tips that we take for granted in the twenty-first century. . . .

- A pre-hunting preparatory step neglected by the majority of hunters: sight in! Or target your rifle on the range as long before you are to take your trip as possible.

- When surf casting in salt water, wet your line before you cast, and you won't have half so many backlashes.

- If you aren't sure if you have caught a smallmouth or largemouth bass, count the rows of scales on the gill covers. A smallmouth has 17 rows, a largemouth 10 rows.

- The woodcock is the slowest flier of all American gamebirds, able to hit 5 mph to 20 mph, depending on how pressed he is. (By comparison, Canada geese can hit 70 mph when they're flying full out!)

- If you touch poison ivy, pour undiluted household ammonia on it as soon as possible. This will kill the ivy acid.

- If it's below zero and your feet are freezing, the surest way to warm them is to take off your boots and socks and dip them in the nearest stream. Even if the air temperature is –20 degrees, the water is never going to be colder than 32 degrees!

Well, you get the idea—and I'm not so sure I'm going to try that last tip. But the point is, this little booklet is now seventy years old, and the tips in here still make sense today, can still make you a better hunter, fisherman, and woodsman. So thumb through the pages, pore over the many illustrations, and then consider how many of these tips you take for granted today—tips that sportsmen of years gone by had never even considered before this landmark book. Then consider this: Perhaps there are tips in here that you have never thought about before . . . and, maybe you should!

Jay Cassell
Editorial Director
Skyhorse Publishing
February 12, 2014

Secrets of Telling One Trout from T'other!

SPOTS!

DOLLY VARDEN RAINBOW

BROWN TROUT BROOK TROUT

American trout are divided into two basic groups, true trout and charrs. On all true trout the spots are darker than the body color, while on charrs the spots are lighter than the body color.

BROOK TROUT

Eastern Brook Trout, often called "Squaretail," "Speckled Trout," or "Red Spot," is a charr.

Red spots along sides, with an irregular lighter color circle surrounding each spot. Front of lower fins pink or red, edged with white. Vermicular, or wavy markings on back, distinguish the brook trout from all others. The tail is square and unforked.

RAINBOW TROUT

Rainbow Trout. A true trout. A wide pink lateral stripe usually identifies the rainbow—but in open lakes with sandy bottoms and in some streams the color is very faint. Spots are black, without surrounding circles of light color, as in the brook, brown, and Dolly Varden. Young rainbows under eight or nine inches are much different in general appearance than adult fish. Nose is blunt and rounded, eye prominent, tail somewhat forked and poorly developed, and the sides are covered with dark blotches or parr markings instead of the rainbow stripe of the grown fish. The adult has sharper nose, small eye, and fairly square tail.

BROWN TROUT

Brown Trout. A true trout. May be distinguished from both the Eastern Brook and the Dolly Varden by the black spots on its back. Although having red spots on the sides, the Brown is unlike the Eastern Brook in its belly fin coloration, the fins lacking the red, edged with white, of the Brook Trout. The Brown has a flat vomer, the bone forming the front part of the roof of the mouth, which is supplied with teeth, while the Brook Trout has a boat shaped vomer, which has no teeth.

DOLLY VARDEN TROUT

Dolly Varden, also called "Western Brook," and "Bull Trout," is the only native Western charr. Resembles both the Eastern Brook and the Laker in general appearance. Tail slightly forked. Spots are red, with background lighter than the body of the fish. Easily distinguished from the Eastern Brook Trout by the lack of vermicular, or "worm-like" wavy markings on the back.

Lake Trout, often called "Laker," "Mackinaw," "Gray Trout," and, in New England, "Togue." Closely related to the charrs, it has spots lighter than the body color. Easily distinguished from the Brook Trout and Brown Trout by the lack of red in the spots. Has no red, pink, or other bright colors.

CUTTHROAT
TROUT

Cutthroat. Readily recognized by a distinct red or crimson V on the throat. Although rainbows have a somewhat similar marking sometimes, it is less distinct, and more pink than bright red. Has a narrow band of small teeth on hyoid bone at base of tongue, which teeth are lacking in the Rainbow, with which some anglers confuse it, due to its black spotted back.

Steelhead. Many anglers refer to both the sea run rainbow and the sea run cutthroat as "rainbows." However, the true steelhead is generally accepted as the rainbow gone to sea. Silvery, and with spots few and indistinct, when fresh run from the sea into Western coastal streams, he lacks the lateral rainbow stripe of pink, but that often comes back later, while he is in fresh water. Distinguished from the sea-run cutthroat by the lack of small teeth on the hyoid bone at the base of the tongue. The head seems smaller in proportion to the fish, and more pointed, than in the strictly fresh water rainbow.

STEELHEAD

Salient Salmon Facts

The Atlantic Salmon and its "landlocked" forms, are the only members of the salmon family native to Eastern America.

Unlike the Pacific salmon, the Atlantic salmon doesn't die after spawning, but returns again and again from the ocean to its native stream for reproduction.

Atlantic salmon, according to most anglers, do not feed while in fresh water, and take the fly only out of

SILVER OR COHO SALMON

ATLANTIC SALMON

LANDLOCKED SALMON

CHINOOK OR TYEE SALMON

curiosity, or playfulness, or anger. Other anglers deny this claim, and maintain that salmon do, and will eat insects, etc., while in streams. These fish, taken on rod and reel, go from five to thirty pounds normally, although fish forty pounds and over are taken every season.

The landlocked salmon and the Ouananiche (pronounced Wah-nah-neesh, with the accent on the first syllable), are both true Atlantic salmon, but do not migrate to the sea, even in lakes connected to it by streams. The "landlocked" was originally native to Maine only, and the "Ouananiche" to the Lake St. John and Saguenay regions of Canada, but both have been transplanted extensively to other regions, in New England and New York. "Landlocks" have also been taken to many lakes in the Midwest and Rocky Mountain States, but on the whole not too successfully. This non-migratory salmon is famous for its gameness, and will take flies, minnows, spoons, and other moving lures.

Anglers may readily distinguish the "landlock" and "Ouananiche" from the Atlantic salmon by its smaller size, chunkier build, darker color, more conspicuous spots, and larger fins and tail in proportion to size.

"Landlocks" generally weigh from 2 pounds up to 7 or 8, although 10 and 12 pounders are sometimes taken. The "Ouananiche" is somewhat smaller, with the maximum 8 to 10 pounds.

The Pacific Chinook or Tyee Salmon is known by many other names, such as king, quinnat, spring, Columbia River, salmon, etc. It is the largest Pacific salmon, often going over forty and fifty pounds, and has been caught weighing over 100 pounds by commercial fishermen, although the rod and reel record is 83 pounds. This salmon is taken by anglers in both salt and fresh water. It dies after spawning in the headwaters of rivers, sometimes 1000 miles from its home in the sea!

The Pacific Silver, or Coho, salmon, remains near the shore while in the ocean, and is the nearest of the Western salmon in appearance and fighting tactics to the Atlantic salmon. Next to the Chinook it is the largest Pacific salmon, and like the former, may be taken on rod and reel in both salt and fresh water. They run from 10 to 20 pounds, and sometimes reach 30 pounds and slightly over. Like all Pacific salmon they die after spawning in fresh water.

Trout Trickers and Takers Extraordinary!

I never met any trout fisherman who had ever used an old and time tested trick I have employed for many years—the "Trout Cocktail." On the first small hook of a trout "worming gang" I put a small cricket or hopper, on the second hook a small wiggly piece of worm, on the third a small chip of cut bait, throat latch of a minnow, small minnow tail, or fish eye.

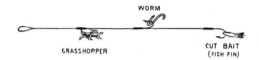

WORM

GRASSHOPPER

CUT BAIT
(FISH FIN)

This, drifted naturally down stream on greased line, ungreased leader, brings 'em out when other methods fail.

Another unorthodox but highly successful fly rig for me is a very small dry fly for a dropper, about three feet above a wet fly or small streamer, fished on a short line.

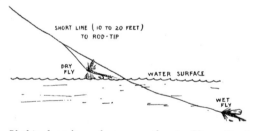

SHORT LINE (10 TO 20 FEET)
TO ROD-TIP

DRY
FLY

WATER SURFACE

WET
FLY

If this doesn't work, reverse the rig. Use a big dry fly for a floater, about eighteen inches, to three feet above a tiny wet fly, on a greased line, floated down from upstream, and allowed to go downstream also, as far as possible. I have taken trout after trout on this rig by striking instantly, at the slightest quiver of the floating fly. In deep pools use from three to five or six feet of light leader between the floater and the wet fly.

Unorthodox though it may seem, many times in retrieving this combination when it has floated down stream, I have had trout hit the big floater on its way up against the current! But far more often, coming upstream, the wet has proved the taking fly. Be prepared for a rise on either fly, however, at any moment.

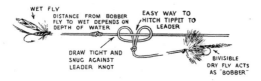

WET FLY
DISTANCE FROM BOBBER
FLY TO WET DEPENDS ON
DEPTH OF WATER
EASY WAY TO
HITCH TIPPET TO
LEADER
DRAW TIGHT AND
SNUG AGAINST
LEADER KNOT
BIVISIBLE
DRY FLY ACTS
AS "BOBBER"

When you are near the seacoast and can keep live salt water shrimp alive on trips to nearby trout streams or lakes you'll find this bait about the most taking one you ever used for any and all kinds of trout. Use an eight or ten hook, with a single shrimp if they're adult size, two on the hook if small, and be sure they're alive and transparent.

Best way to keep shrimp alive is to pack a basket (large grape basket) with sawdust and ice, and place only a couple of gills of shrimp, in burlap wet with sea water, folded up around the shrimp and laid flat on the sawdust, but not touching the ice.

This, of course, is for boat fishing, or fishing from landings. When stream fishing use a small paper ice cream box with flap covers, packed with sawdust and ice, with holes in the sides and bottom to allow draining off ice water, and shrimps in sea water wet burlap at the top. Tie in such a way in your creel that box can't tip over.

Shrimp are, when transparent and alive, one of the world's best baits also for both kinds of bass, landlock salmon, and white perch. Yellow perch, blue gills and horn pout will take them eagerly when white, and absolutely dead.

Hook shrimp through the tails to keep them liveliest. This is a delicate job—be careful to hook from the inside of the curving tail right out through the outside of the bend, just once, leaving hook point projecting.

COONS ARE SO CURIOUS that some trappers hang glittering objects over traps for bait, and rely on the coon investigating and stepping into the trap.

Trout Tricks That Tally!

The Mud Ball

If there's a big brown or brook trout that resists all
your cajoling, try this, and chances are mighty good
you'll land him.

Mix up some wet earth and clay into a stiff paste..
Surround a good lively night crawler, or worm, that
you have hooked lightly, with a ball of this. Lower it
silently into the pool or deep spot where the big fish
lurks. Then keep quiet, holding your rod motionless.
The current will wash the mud and earth off, and the
worm will emerge by degrees and wiggles. No hungry
trout, suspicious or not, can withstand such a perfectly
natural presentation of a perfect snack!

The Dropping Worm or Fly

Hook worm as shown, so that the hook won't catch
on the grass or branches. Then make a very gentle
cast, stopping the bait above the grass or branches that
overhang the deep part of the pool, and allowing it to
fall gently. Wait. Count sixty, keeping absolutely
motionless. Then gently pull the worm off into the
water. If there's a trout present he'll grab it!

The bait falls into the water much more naturally
than when you drop it in direct, or let it drift down.
Besides, you allow everything to quiet down, and make
no quick or alarming motions.

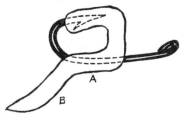

There's a trick to not getting "hung up" on grass or
branches in this kind of fishing. Don't do it on windy
or gusty days. Size up each individual "lie" of the worm,
and gently flick it off from the easiest direction. If the
bait dangles you can often gently lower your rod tip,
and the worm will slide right down into the water. If it
doesn't, just take up the dangling line by slowly raising
the rod tip till only an inch or so dangles. A quick

twitch will then, nine times out of ten, drop the worm into the water.

You can use exactly the same procedure with dry flies—particularly bivisibles—and with even less probability of getting "hung up" on branches or grass.

The Floating Branch

Cut a small green branch with a leaf or two on it. Hook your worm or fly very lightly through a leaf, as close to the edge as possible. Let the branch and lure float downstream way under the overhanging bushes, where you can't cast. Twitch the hook free from the leaf, and your worm will sink most naturally down where a hungry trout will grab it. If you use a fly you can retrive it with short jerks and pauses, and get many a rise by this method! And you can place your lure where you can't possibly get it under low hanging branches by any other method.

HOOK LEAF VERY LIGHTLY
CLOSE TO THE EDGE AS POSSIBLE

Worm Tipped Fly

When the trout are rising and won't take your wet or dry flies, try a very tiny wet fly on which you have hooked the end of the tail of a small worm . . . just a small piece, not more than an eighth to a quarter inch long. Cast this as usual, and retrieve on, or just under, the surface.

When fishing a run, or slow flowing pool, cast upstream, and allow the lure to drift down with the current. Strip in slack and be ready to strike on the least flash, or the slightest suspicion of line movement.

Reversed Minnow Trick

When every other bait you try fails for big browns, brook trout, Dolly Vardens, cutthroats, rainbows and even steelheads and landlock salmon, try this reversed minnow. See the drawing for all the details. When your minnow is properly "sewed on" by this method, put an eighth to half ounce sinker on the leader three to four feet up the leader. Then manipulate your lure and sinker into a pool or near a big rock or bunch of rocks. Allow the sinker to go right on down to the bottom. The current makes the minnow just waver from side to side, without spinning, and for some reason, stirs up the big fish into an irresistible desire to grab your lure! Having tried this method with great success on Western streams I have modified it for slow deep trolling in Eastern lakes, and have been amazed at the number of lakers, squaretails, and landlocks it has caught.

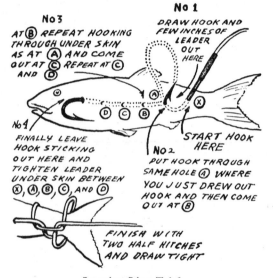

Leaping Line Trick

On a windy day stand still in one position and let the wind carry your fly out. "Dap" and skip it everywhere you can. Work always with the wind, letting it carry your fly out to cover a complete group of imaginary semi-circles, A, B, C, etc.

First let the wind carry the fly to 1, then lower the rod tip and drop the fly on the water. Tighten the line, and the wind will lift the fly from the water. Then lower the tip and the fly will strike the water at 2. Let it hit the water again at 3, and so on, as far as the wind will take it. You can then work it back toward you a foot or so to the left, always keeping it "dapping" and dancing, on the surface, till you have covered all the water in front of you. This method will often bring up fish on a windy day when no other way of presenting the fly seems to work.

You can vary the "dapping" and skipping by slacking line, letting the fly drop to the surface, then gradually tightening the line till the wind makes the fly skid and slide and skip along the surface. This, too, is a mighty taking way of getting rises, on a windy day.

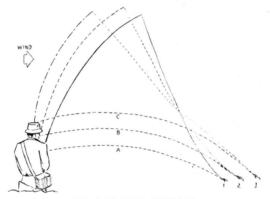

SKETCHES FROM OUTDOORS

To Keep Fish All Summer

Boil water enough to cover the fish, and while still hot add salt until the brine will float a fresh egg. Cool. Put in the fish. Weigh them down beneath the surface with stones. The fish will become very salty, and will need plenty of freshening in clear water before cooking.

Smoked fish will keep as well, and are more palatable to most fishermen. Cut into halves. Remove entrails and heads. Soak overnight in strong brine described above. Remove and hang up to drain four or five hours. Then smoke by hanging on wires in a wooden box with tight fitting bottom and top, the latter removable. The smoke pipe from a small stove enters the box at the bottom at the extreme right, and a hole to permit draft is made in the bottom at the extreme left. In other words the smoke intake and exit are as far apart as possible. Use green apple, birch, or willow wood, or dampen dry wood, to produce a rich smoke. Smoke eight hours. Then dry out for 30 or 40 minutes with a hotter fire. Cool, and store in a cool, dry place, with layers of paper between layers of fish and each fish slightly separated from every other.

How to Pick Your Pike, Pickerel, Muskellunge, and "Pike-Perch"

Look at the pictures on page 16 and 17 carefully, and you'll see immediately that one fish has an entirely different arrangement and structure of the fins. That one, top fish page 16, is a "pike-perch" or "wall-eyed pike." Note the spines in its dorsal, or back fin. None of the others have these spines.

Better get the habit of calling this fish a "wall-eye," because the eyes are its most outstanding difference from all other fresh water fishes. They are very large, much larger than in pickerel, pike, or musky, and have a whitish, translucent glow, peculiar to walleyes alone.

Pickerel, pike, and musky look a lot alike to the untrained eye, but the experienced angler can generally tell them apart without closely examining the gill covers and cheecks for their characteristic distribution of scales (see illustration on page 15).

In the first place, pickerel are considerably smaller than pike—better call pike "Great Northerns," as most anglers do, and avoid confusing them with wall-eyed "pike." Pickerel rarely reach six or seven pounds weight—the average is around 1½ lbs. to 2½. A three pounder is a really large pickerel, and four and five pounders are distinctly uncommon. On the other hand, Great Northerns and Muskellunge from ten pounds up to fifteen and twenty pounds are not at all unusual. Pickerel are more yellowish green than pike, which have light colored, bean shaped blotches on a green background. The pickerel has chain shaped markings (reticulations), while the muskellunge has the least vivid markings of all—showing only an alternate vague stripe of lighter and darker effect. These stripes seem to merge into the body color and are not very vivid—in many muskies being almost or quite absent.

The One Sure Way to Tell 'Em Apart

Note from the detailed drawings at right that the muskellunge (top) has the gill covers (opercles) and cheeks, both entirely without scales on their lower halves.

The Great Northern Pike (second drawing down) has the cheeks entirely scaled, while the opercles are not scaled on their lower halves.

But the pickerel (bottom sketch) has both gill covers and cheeks entirely scaled.

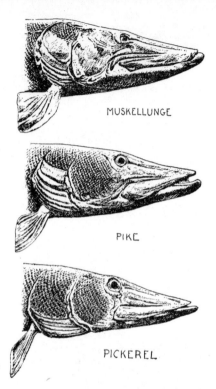

MUSKELLUNGE

PIKE

PICKEREL

Besides the above infallible method of distinguishing pickerel, pike, and musky, the pike and pickerel may be readily differentiated if you will remember that pickerel have a general effect of green markings laid on over yellow, while the pike gives the effect of yellow over green.

The largest pickerel ever caught weighed a little over ten pounds, and although a Great Northern weighing nearly 46 pounds, and a 62½ pound musky have been taken, the average weight of all three fish taken by anglers is very much lower.

Pike and Pickerel "Pointers"

One of the most irritating of all pike and pickerel traits is their habit of following a bait long distances without striking it.

However, there are one or two tricks worth knowing, in this connection, which will tease these fish into action. For example, I always keep the lure in motion right up to the very boat itself, and, instead of making a quick motion to lift it out, at the end of the retrieve, just keep it going a foot or two further by stripping in more line on fly rod lures, or reeling in a few more turns when bait casting. The main points here are to keep the lure in the water the extra instant or two necessary for the fish to strike before the bait escapes, and to guard against any sudden movement that may alarm your quarry. Slowly lifting the bait to the surface will often bring that precious last second strike, so startling, and yet so valuable often in making the trip a success—provided you school yourself to take advantage of it when it comes. Nothing is so disconcerting as losing fish which strike unbelievably close to the boat—as they often will, if you follow the method outlined above, and are not ready for the rise.

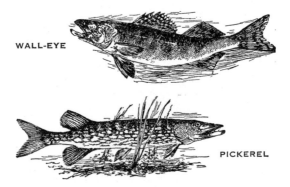

WALL-EYE

PICKEREL

If you see a pike or pickerel following your lure cast back into the water a few feet, with the easiest motion possible, and retrieve, without any quick movements, or alarming maneuvers of the rod. Often the fish will come back in a savage, determined strike.

If you can't tease your pike or pickerel to strike the first time you cast back to him, try retrieving faster the second time. Often a speedier retrieve seems to excite these fish into action.

Another "exciter" is a change of bait. When bait or fly casting, if you have one or two strips of perch, or pickerel, belly all cut and wrapped in damp cloth, with the hook already in place, you can quickly snap this bait on your casting swivel, and toss it out a few feet

"MUSKY"

GREAT NORTHERN

from your boat where a pike or pickerel has followed your previous lure in. Allowing this to sink down, and slowly retrieving to the top of the water, and the boat, will often bring a determined strike.

Speaking of a change of bait, the popping or whirling surface bait will often bring pike and pickerel to the top of the water in surging, savage strikes, when the underwater plug or spoon has failed, after several tries.

And speaking of a change of pace, a perch, pickerel, or sunfish belly, allowed to sink, and retrieved in very slow, short jerks, will often bring strikes where the same lure, "skittered" as usual near the surface and at a faster pace will utterly fail. By the same token, if slowly retrieved baits fail, the fast recovery is worth trying, as detailed above.

The natural, and the best, places to look for pike and pickerel are in coves, where lily pads, pickerel weeds, or other aquatic growths abound. At times, if they are absent from such natural feeding grounds, where perch, minnows, other small fry and frogs disport, you'll find them along the shore line leading to the coves and bends, or in slightly deeper water where there are sunken weed beds, or patches of growth.

Steelhead and Salmon

One Secret of Saving 'Em After You Snag 'Em!

My experience with the long shank hook, as I set forth and illustrated in a recent issue of "Hunting and Fishing," has always been that it is more apt to tear out, through leverage, than the extremely short shank hook. The article referred to was concerned with bass, but the principle there explained holds good especially for such persistent, enduring, dogged, and brilliant fighters as Atlantic, Pacific, and landlocked Salmon, as well as steelhead and sea run cutthroats.

Therefore, for the last few years, I have been tying flies and streamers on the "short, short" shank type of hook, as well as using it for baiting.

For another reason the "short, short" shank is best: Where a small hook, with fine calibre wire, will cut through bone and gristle, under the persistent pull and shaking of a heavy, active fish, the "short, short" shank, larger in size, with a larger diameter wire—will hold far better, far longer.

FLY TIED ON #6 ORDINARY HOOK

SAME SIZE FLY TIED ON "SHORT, SHORT" SHANK #2 HOOK

For instance, without making the fly appear larger, you can use the same volume of feathers on a number four or two hook with the extra short shank that you would use on a long shank, or ordinary shank, six or eight hook,—and the four, or two, will have a lot deeper "bite" and bend, as well as a bigger diameter of wire, without additional weight or aggregate bulk.

I will say this, also, for the short, short shank hook used with flies or streamers: the shank being shorter, is taken well past the lips on the strike, and is held longer in the mouth of the fish before being ejected, since it doesn't strike the lips, as a longer shank would. This is important, especially with dry flies, where the fish will often hold short, short shank flies long enough to turn and start down with them—and where, when using the upstream cast and "drift fly" with sunken flies, the momentary retention of the fly by the fish means giving the angler a little more chance to strike and hook the fish.

With bait, the short, short shank has manifest advantages. It is easier to "sew on" than long shank hooks —doesn't tear the minnow, and manipulates far easier. In bait, too, it is far less conspicuous.

My advice, therefore, to the Pacific, as well as the Atlantic angler, is to have your flies tied on "short, short" shank hooks, and to use these same hooks whenever you employ live or trolled minnows. Where you would normally use a number six, eight, or ten long shank hook, you can use two, three, or four size short, short shank hooks.

While it is true that with dry flies they won't ride as high and prettily with too large a hook, it is still possible by using a little judgment in balancing the hackle with the weight of the hook, to tie a fly that will float nicely cocked-up on the water.

Certainly, the sinking quality of wet flies on the larger "short, short" hook is quite as good as on the smaller long shank, and the balance is better, since more weight comes below the feathers and causes the fly to drift, or retrieve, in an upright position—a position much better, by the way, for sure hooking when you sink the hook home.

Compare both flies. Note that the one tied with the same amount of feathers and shorter body on #2 hook doesn't look larger than the one tied on the longer shank #6 hook.

Are Porcupines Edible?

If a porcupine be slowly simmered for several hours when cut up for a stew with onions and other vegetables it is mighty good eating. If roasted, it should be parboiled from 30 to 50 minutes previous to putting in the oven.

IMPORTANT—Most Important

If you fish with streamer flies, fly rod lures, or perch belly, for pike and pickerel, the wire leader, unless it is far lighter than most, ruins the action, and will materially cut down on your strikes. The ordinary casting trace of wire is an abomination and a redundance. Substitute for it a double six to nine inch length of heavy bait casting line—about 40 to 45 pounds test. This line is so flexible it allows plenty of action to any lure, and the loosely braided, soft silk line allows the sharp teeth of the fish to sink between the strands, without cutting them. Perhaps this sounds like wishful thinking—but experience has shown me that if the two strands of line are each fastened individually to the lure, if one is severed, the other will hold. And the action of the plug, or wobbling spoon, or natural bait, or fly, is so much more attractive, that even if an occasional bite-off occurs, the strikes are far more numerous.

If you fear "bite-offs" with the above rig, use a very light wire, like a violin E string.

Inside Information on Locating Landlocks

Look for landlocked salmon, when the ice goes out, about twenty to forty feet off shore, and around the ledges.

From a few days to two weeks later, they will be found, in lakes where smelt abound, around the mouths of the streams and along the bars at the mouths of streams where the smelt are coming back into the lake from their Spring spawning runs. Here will be found the most fast and furious landlocked fishing of all.

A number eight or six streamer will then do grand execution. So will live, or trolled, minnows or smelt. The best streamers at this time seem to be the Supervisor, Black Ghost, Gray Ghost, Green Ghost, Governor Aiken, St. John, white and blue Maribou, and others very closely resembling smelts in their action and sheen. I have had remarkable results, at these locations, with slender strips of cut bait from chubs or whitefish, fished exactly as one would "skitter" for pickerel, allowing the bait, on the cast, to sink nearly to the bottom, then playing up, in slow jerks. At these spots still-fished live bait will secure strike after strike —and so will top-trolled streamers, and spinners, either with smelt, flies, or worms.

In late May, or early June, around Memorial Day, the salmon seem to scatter all over the lake, and some wonderful fly fishing is possible off the ledges and around the sunken rocks off shore.

I recommend a little "prospecting" the year before, with definite notes, and landmarks jotted down on paper, locating likely spots, where you have taken salmon, or where the underwater formations look likely. For instance, I have repeatedly located spots where the rocks furnished cover to minnows, and where there were open spaces surrounded by rocks, then come back next season, or next day, and cast a fly, or lightly tossed a minnow—with immediate and thrilling results. Salmon seem to lurk around such places, occasionally dashing into the groups of small fish and picking up a meal for themselves. Fly casting along the shore at this time is generally profitable and so is surface trolling with a streamer, smelt, minnow, or stickleback.

A deadly combination at this time, and until the salmon go into deep water at the end of June, is a Silver Gray, Jock Scott, or Black Dose Atlantic Salmon fly, about size six, and a very small minnow or smelt hooked on behind it, through the nose.

MINNOW-
AND-
STREAMER
COMBINATION

After the last of June you will ordinarily have to fish deeper, slow trolling with a long line and sinker, or drifting along with live bait, or small deeply sunken pieces of cut bait (where such fishing is legal).

There are certain cold spring holes, however, where, if you are familiar with your lake, you can catch salmon all Summer, at depths varying from medium to deep (thirty to about eighty feet).

About the first of September the landlock will come back into comparatively shallow water again, and you can use about the same tactics and lures as in the Spring. However, this September fishing seems to be either mighty good or mighty poor. Some years I have found it wonderful—others terrible. I think a lot depends on knowing your lake—or having a good guide who knows it.

What Proportion of Deer are Shot?

According to the California Fish and Game Commission one hunter gets his buck while two and six-tenths don't!

The Expert's Secret Flies Are Now Public Property

According to a secret ballot, sent with proper publicity, by "Hunting and Fishing" to twenty of the country's best known fishermen, the best flies for trout (s-s-sh-h-h-) are:

Wet flies—
1. Coachman. 2. Brown Hackle. 3. Dark Montreal.

Dry flies—
1. Bivisible (brown and gray—take your choice).
2. Fanwing Royal Coachman.
3. Cahill.
4. Quill Gordon.

Streamers—
1. Black Ghost.
2. Light (or Yellow) Tiger.
3. Brown Bucktail.

So-o-o, if you haven't been getting your quota of trout, why not stock up with two or three sizes of each of the above—then go out and conquer?

Large Mouth, Small Mouth, or Rock Bass?

The surest way to tell whether a bass is a large mouth or a small mouth is to count the rows of scales on the gill covers. If there are 17 rows, it's a small mouth, if 10 rows a large mouth. Then to be doubly sure, count the rows of scales from the front back fin to the median line (that's a line you can see along the side of most all bass). The small mouth has 11 rows of scales here, the large mouth only 7.

Most experienced anglers can tell from a glance at the maxillary bone (the one that rims the upper jaw) whether a bass is the small or large mouth variety. The small mouth's maxillary extends to an imaginary vertical line through the eye. On the large mouth the maxillary extends back beyond this imaginary vertical line through the eye.

In general, the small mouth is a trimmer, more streamlined fish than the large mouth, and the scales seem a bit smaller. The large mouth, as he grows larger and heavier, has a tendency to develop a paunch, while the small mouth keeps his trim figure far better.

The rock bass is easy to distinguish from the large or small mouth, as he seldom grows beyond a pound or

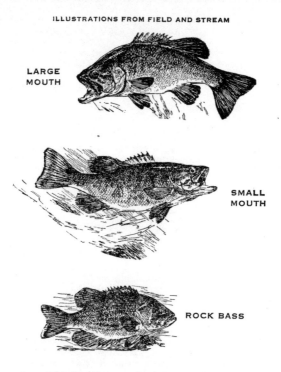

LARGE
MOUTH

SMALL
MOUTH

ROCK BASS

so in weight, has larger scales in proportion to his size, and has more spines on the anal fin (the fin extending from the vent back toward the tail).

Plumb Lining for Small Mouths

The basis for getting right down to the territory where the small mouth bass goes foraging for his food is to have a heavy sinker, say two to four ounces, on a sturdy line, and use this for feeling out and sounding out the bottom.

Small mouths like to feed along rocky bars and ledges that shelve off into deep water, and on sand-and-rocky underwater plateaus at the mouths of coves, and in rocky coves, and along rocky shores, where the minnows and crawfish lurk.

Tie some cloth, or different colored strings, at various depths on your sounding line. Put one at ten feet, another at twelve, another at fourteen, and so on, with a marker, easily memorized and recognized, at each depth up to about thirty feet.

You will generally find your small mouths in water from six or seven feed deep down to about thirty feet. And, throughout the season, into latest October and November, in from ten to twenty feet of water in the daytime.

At night the small mouth can be found in much shallower water, in coves, and along the rocky shore line, and on the ledges and bars, often in from two to six or seven feet of water.

Some of the best small mouth fishing is to be found where there are occasional patches of underwater weeds scattered here and there over rocky ledges, sandy bars, or level reaches at the mouths of coves, from seven or eight to twelve feet deep.

HELGRAMITE (FINE BAIT FOR BASS)

By sounding with your lead, you can tell the depth and character of the water. Generally it is wise to move on somewhere else if the bottom seems muddy, and nine times out of ten, during the Summer days, you'll locate bass somewhere in the ten to twenty foot depths.

One of the useful purposes of your plumb line will be to reveal at what depth you ought to sink your bait. In general, you should fish a foot off the bottom, but sometimes, with helgramites, frogs, and crayfish, especially when over a sandy bar, where your bait can't crawl under a rock, you'll have better luck right down on the bottom. If the foot-off-the-bottom system doesn't work, try on-the-bottom fishing. Crayfish, helgramites, and small frogs, however, will creep under rocks, on rocky bottoms, so you'll find it best to use bottom fishing only on sand or gravel.

One of the best ways to get small mouths is to anchor on a ledge, if the wind is blowing off it, and, if the bass don't bite at ten or twelve feet, pay out a few yards of anchor line and drift into deeper water—fourteen, then sixteen, then eighteen, then twenty, and so on, till you find bass. Or, if the wind blows toward the ledge, anchor way off it in deep water, and gradually let the wind work your boat into shallower water, till you hit the depth where bass are feeding.

You'll get many more bites on light tackle than on heavy leaders and large hooks. Use "short short" shank hooks, and nylon leaders of six pounds test or less.

For sinkers use two "BB's" or a single buckshot. Avoid big, heavy, unwieldly sinkers. Also avoid large hooks, especially long shanked ones. A number six or eight will hold the biggest small mouth that swims, and you'll get twice or three times the bites on small hooks and light leaders.

When using minnows for bait, however, a number four hook is about right, as the smaller hooks often slide right out of the bass' mouth and throat with the minnow, when you try to set the hook—the minnow shielding too small a hook and preventing the point from entering the bass.

Fish for bass after dark with floating bugs and plugs. Grease your line for the former, so you won't pull the bug under water when you retrieve it, or when you row slowly along (yes, very slowly—just *creep*) with about forty feet of line out behind your boat.

I have found two types of bugs, the "popping" type, with balsa or cork body, and deer hair tail and fins, and the all deer hair floating bug, the best at night. Sometimes a wiggly feather tail, on a deer hair body bug, is the most effective night lure you can possibly use.

One of the best natural baits for bass is the helgramite. You can keep them lively and full of wiggle by putting them in a box, from which light is excluded, with dead, damp leaves, or rotten wood, or a piece of damp burlap, or sod, or ground-moss from which the earth has been well shaken.

Minnows can best be kept alive and full of pep by placing in water in a wooden bucket, or one of those wooden butter tubs. There's something about these receptacles which keeps them kicking for hours.

Do You Know That . . .

Newborn Opossums are so tiny that you could put more than 100 in the scales to balance the weight of a silver dollar. Grown up, these identical mites of animals may weigh from ten to fourteen pounds each!

Black Squirrels are only "melanistic" phases of the common gray squirrel!

Foxes have elliptical eye-pupils, like cats, when contracted, while dogs and wolves' eye pupils are always round.

Raccoons rarely attain over 30 pounds in weight. The rumor that they reach 50 or 60 pounds is apparently not founded on fact, according to Biological Survey records.

Secret of Catching Pout
Without Hooks

Take narrow strips of calico rags and wind them into a ball about an inch in diameter. Roughly stitch these together with thread. Loop one end of a leader around this rag ball, and stitch the leader firmly to it.

Then, with a needle, thread worms on a good strong linen thread, and wind the worms and thread around the ball, till the whole is about two inches or so in diameter.

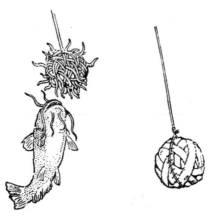

THE "WORM BALL" FOR POUT

Let this down to the bottom, and when you feel a nibble pull it up gently, slowly, and gradually till you see it near the surface. Then give a quick lift into the boat, together with the pout, sometimes two, or three, clinging to the worm and thread. Touch the pouts' tails to a pail, or a metal pan, and they'll let go. Lower your worm ball, and repeat.

To make "bull-pout" most palatable, here is a cooking secret worth knowing.

After cleaning and skinning, score them on the sides right down to the backbone as shown in the sketch.

Then rub in some flour and cornmeal mixed and fry in bacon grease, lard, or vegetable oil.

The secret of well cooked bull-pout is to cook slowly at first, then crisp and brown the outside with a hotter fire.

If your pout are to be eaten next morning they'll taste better if you put your evening's catch, after dressing, into well salted water and let them soak all night. In the morning score lightly—not as heavily as shown in the sketch—and cook as described above.

Pout make a very fine chowder. After dressing put the whole fish into just enough lightly salted water to cover them. While boiling for about half an hour at a simmer, fry some onions and small chunks of salt pork. Remove bones, and put the onions and pork into the kettle with the fish. Add half a can of evaporated milk, and a few common crackers. Simmer for fifteen minutes. Then serve.

For about two pounds of pout, use three or four fair sized onions and about a quarter of a pound of salt pork.

The secret of a good chowder is plenty of onions, the richness of the evaporated milk, and not using too much water.

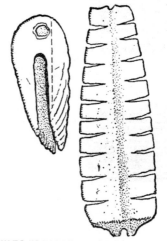

HOW TO "SCORE" POUT FOR COOKING

How Much Do Moose Weigh?

A 1,200 pound moose is a big one—exceptionally big. Even a half-ton moose is really large, but some horses tip the scales at 2,300 or more pounds. But moose definitely top horses in height at the shoulders, a six-foot six, or even a seven foot moose being not at all rare.

Big Game Weighed by Small Fishing Scale

Balance a pole, each end of equal length (this is important) on a tree crotch. Hang the deer, bear, or other big game, on one end, and a bag of stones on the other, till they balance. Then weigh the stones, one or two at a time, with the small scale, and add up the total. This will be the animal's total weight also.

Trout Average Avoirdupois by Inches

Trout increase 2 oz. per inch from 9 to 11 inches, a nine incher weighing 5 oz. and an 11 incher weighing 9 oz.

A 14 inch trout weighs approximately	1 lb. 3 oz.
A 17 inch trout weighs approximately	2 lb. 2 oz.
A 20 inch trout weighs approximately	3 lb. 7 oz.
A 23 inch trout weighs approximately	5 lb. 3 oz.
A 26 inch trout weighs approximately	7 lb. 8 oz.
A 30 inch trout weighs approximately	11 lb. 9 oz.

TROUT

THE MALLARD is one of the slowest flying of all ducks. His cruising speed is about 50 miles per hour, his top speed when pressed 55 to 60 miles per hour.

Fish Weight by Formula

Formula No. 1. A smallmouth bass can be "weighed by rule." Multiply the length in inches by the square of the girth and divide by 55, which gives the weight in ounces, very closely, within an ounce usually for bass up to three pounds. For fish above three pounds, however, this formula goes haywire!

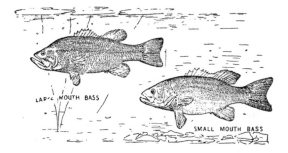

LARGE MOUTH BASS

SMALL MOUTH BASS

Formula No. 2. This works nicely with most fish except bass. Square the girth and multiply by the length in inches. Divide by 800 and you'll have the weight in pounds. Measure from the end of the lower jaw to the fork in the tail.

Atlantic Salmon Weight by Measure

30" weighs 11.5 lbs. approximately.

From 30" to 34" the weight increases 1 lb. 2 oz., 1 lb. 3 oz., 1 lb. 4 oz., and 1 lb. 5 oz., respectively, for each inch in added length, a 34" salmon being 5 lbs. heavier than a 30 incher.

From 35 inches to 40 inches the ratio of increased weight per additional inch in length is about a pound 7 ounces for 36 inches, a pound 8 ounces for 37 inches, a pound 9 ounces for 38 inches, a pound 10 ounces for 39 inches, and two pounds for 40 inches, a 40 incher weighing about 27 pounds 4 ounces.

Banishing Bass Bogies

When every usual method of taking smallmouths meets only cold disdain it's time to revolutionize your approach.

I have made limit catches in the early morning when the bass have been absent from their usual ledges and runs over rocky bottoms and among the rocks, by simply looking for them in their next best hunting grounds, hard sandy plateaus, or level, rocky and sandy stretches, well spotted with underwater weeds.

A lively crawfish or Helgramite weighted down with two small "B B" shot a foot and a half up the leader, hooked through the tail with a #6 Eagle Claw will produce strike after strike. Give plenty of line, take plenty of time, after the strike, till you set the hook. No need to let the bait down on the bottom, as at times like this in from eight to twelve feet of water, as you drift along, the crawfish are seized at all heights.

Another unusual procedure for bass on windy days, when every other method fails, is to anchor in ten to fifteen feet of water, and let your bait, weighted by two buckshot go right down on the bottom of hard sand.

As the boat sways in the wind, your bait, dragged on the bottom, often will stir smallmouths to desperation, and they'll nail it savagely against the bottom.

If this doesn't work, adopt the opposite extreme. Put on a leader with no sinker, and swing your light bait, a cricket, shrimp, Helgramite, or hopper, out on the wind as far as  you can. On fly rods and eight or nine foot boat rods this will easily be eighteen to twenty-five feet from the boat. There the slowly sinking bait will drag through the water close to the top as the boat swings about in the wind, and produce plenty of bites.

On very windy days, if you are careful not to thump the boat bottom, this long light line fishing will get results in from three to six feet of water in coves near lily pads, or offshore among rocks, or on the two foot to six foot shallows near rocks, on the ledges rising up in the lake.

For big mouths I have generally found that if you can't seem to get them near the edge of the pads, reeds, rushes, or pickerel weed, you can induce savage smashes by using weedless pork chunks, weedless frog harness, or weedless dead minnow rigs, right on and among the thickest of water growths. You'll be surprised at the way the big boys burst like bombs right up through a carpet of thick weeds. Pickerel belly strips, or perch, or sunfish chunks, cut out of the throat "V" and four inches down the belly, rigged on weedless long shank hooks, are also good producers on thick or fairly thick weed beds.

Try live salt water shrimp, on four to six pound test leaders and #6 Eagle Claw Hooks, special short shanks. See "Trout Trickers and Takers Extraordinary" for directions complete on keeping and hooking shrimp.

Natural Bait Riddles Solved!

To Preserve Minnows

Put them in a wide necked bottle in which you have a 3% solution of Formalin. Minnows will be a little stiff after staying very long in this simple solution.

Another formula is ½ oz. Formalin, 3 oz. Glycerine, 20 oz. water. Keep shiners in this a month, then remove and keep in strong salt water brine till you need them. This removes the Formalin odor, and keeps bait indefinitely and not so stiff.

Catching Plenty of Grasshoppers

Wait till after dark, then go out with a flashlight, and you can pick off grasshoppers from the grass and leaves by the dozens, where you have hard work chasing them and catching them in the daytime. At night they obligingly stay quiescent in the flashlight rays!

To Keep Crayfish

Two bait dealers I know near Boston keep Crayfish fresh and lively by simply putting enough water in tubs, or pails, to partly cover the crayfish. About an inch and a half to two inches of water is about right. Soft water, or rain water, in an open wooden trough, with protective wire netting (fine mesh) is an ideal set-up for keeping this good bass bait. The smaller ones about two and a half to three and a half inches are best.

Some Worm Getters

Save your walnut shells, and soak them in enough water to cover, for several days, stirring them up a bit now and then. Find the little worm mounds in garden, on paths, or on the lawn, make a little hollow in each and put a tablespoonful or so of your walnut solution in each. If you keep refilling each hole now and then the worms will come out quickly and you can collect 'em!

Another good worm producing "lotion" is a weak solution of dry mustard powder and water poured into their holes.

Go out at night, particularly when it's damp, dewy, or drizzly, and you can pick up night crawlers by the dozen with the aid of a flashlight.

Often after a cool damp night, when a little rain has fallen, or the dew is heavy, you can find plenty of worms right after dawn on the wet macadam roads. The black headed worm found in garden soil is the best of all bait worms.

Cricket Lore

You'll find this best of all smallmouth bass bait by getting down on your hands and knees and hunting through the grass for them. You have to look  closely. If no luck in the grass (not the short grass of lawns, but field grass) you'll usually find them under old tar paper, boards, timbers, flat stones, etc., that rest on the ground near fields.

You can keep them from eating each other by putting a leaf of lettuce for them to eat, in your container, as well as a wad of grass or leaves for them to range around in. A bit of bone meal sprinkled in now and then is good food for them.

June Bugs for Bass

Don't let the June bugs that K. O. themselves against screens, window panes and light globes go to waste. Collect 'em, and use 'em next day for bass.

If you can gather 'em alive on your screens, where they're attracted by lights, they're all the better. Both large and smallmouth bass are crazy for June Bugs.

Mysteries of Cleaning and Keeping Fish Revealed!

Dressing Trout with Two Cuts!

Cut No. 1. Hold your trout by the back. Insert the point of a sharp knife in the vent and slit up lengthwise through middle of the stomach in a straight line from the vent to the "V" between the gills.

Cut No. 2. Insert the knife crosswise under the lower jaw, entering under the "V" shaped cartilage on the right and coming out on the left side. The knife should enter as far back just ahead of the gill rim as possible. Cut the cartilage away from the front end of the jaw.

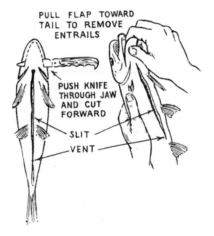

PULL FLAP TOWARD TAIL TO REMOVE ENTRAILS

PUSH KNIFE THROUGH JAW AND CUT FORWARD

SLIT

VENT

No further cuts are necessary. Simply upend the trout, holding the jaw in the left hand, and the cartilage, gills, and forward (pectoral) fins in the right. Pull downward, and out come gills, cartilage and entrails in one complete operation.

That's all there is to it. But if you're very finicky you can run the thumb nail or knife blade up and down the backbone to remove the blood accumulated there. Also you can scrape the fish to remove surplus "lubrication."

No More "Muddy" Pickerel!

Chief cause of a "muddy taste" in pickerel is the copious protective slime in the skin. Therefore, after scaling keep on with the same motion, repeatedly scraping away the mucous coating till you can scrape away no more! Then cut off the head, slit the belly, remove the entrails and the blood along the backbone, and you have a particularly toothsome, sweet flavored fish—without the least vestige of "muddy" taste.

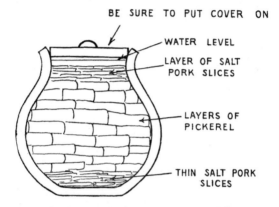

BE SURE TO PUT COVER ON

WATER LEVEL

LAYER OF SALT PORK SLICES

LAYERS OF PICKEREL

THIN SALT PORK SLICES

If pickerel bones bother you cut your fish up into inch thick cross sections, put a layer of thin salt pork slices on the bottom of a bean pot, put in a few layers of pickerel, then top layers of salt pork slices, cover with water, put on the bean pot cover, and bake from five to seven hours in a slow oven. The bones will be soft as the salmon bones in canned salmon, and you can crunch 'em down with absolutely no bother at all!

———— ★ ————

"Boiling Off" The Skin

Place the whole fish in boiling water. Keep it there, entirely submerged, while leisurely counting 40, if the fish weighs from one to two pounds. Any fish from 2 pounds and up should be submerged in boiling water ten counts longer for each additional pound up to five pounds. After that 70 counts is enough for any fish, but generally you can't use this method, anyway, for fish above 5 pounds, as you won't have a kettle big enough!

The foregoing applies to all fresh water fish.

Salt water fish need a little longer boiling water immersion. Use 50 counts for one to two pounds, then 10 counts more for each added pound.

After removing from the boiling water pull fins out by the roots, then with a slit down the backbone and one down the belly, head to tail, peel the skin off, easily as peeling a banana. Complete by cutting off head and cleaning out the inside.

How to Dress Bass

Lay either small or largemouth flat on board or stump, slit down the entire length of the back fin and the ventral fin. Turn the fish over and slit down the other side of each fin. Keep the cuts as close to the fins as possible and make them deep, so you can next pull out the fins easily.

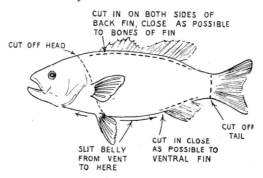

CUT IN ON BOTH SIDES OF
BACK FIN, CLOSE AS POSSIBLE
TO BONES OF FIN

CUT OFF HEAD

CUT OFF TAIL

SLIT BELLY
FROM VENT
TO HERE

CUT IN CLOSE
AS POSSIBLE TO
VENTRAL FIN

Next slit the belly lengthwise from vent to between the gills, cut off the head and grasping it in one hand and holding the fish in the other, pull out the entrails. Clean out the membranes remaining, also the blood along the backbone. Cut off the tail when this is all finished.

Then holding the fish in the hand, left side up, separate the top corner of the skin from the meat and run the thumb along between the skin and the meat down the entire length of the slit you made alongside the back fin. You'll find the skin separates easily, the entire distance, for about an inch in from the edge of the slit.

Then you can easily pull off the entire side of skin. Turn the bass over and repeat on the other side.

Method No. 1. Dress them immediately after catching if possible. Remove gills and all traces of entrails and blood along the backbone. Don't wash the fish in water, but wipe it out with grass or a dry cloth.

Stuff with dry grass, or oiled paper. Don't put away in air-tight bags or creels, or rubber lined receptacles or pockets. Place in willow creel, or other place where air can circulate. Put on ice, after wrapping each fish separately in oiled paper as soon as you reach camp or home.

Method No. 2. Dress immediately, if possible, removing gills, blood, entrails. Wash in water thoroughly. Put a layer damp watercress, lily pads, forget-me-not leaves, or any water plants, in the creel, lay fish on top. Keep fish separated with water-growths. Don't use green grass as this heats up. Occasionally sprinkle the water-growth. Water plants keep cool, anyway, and the evaporation intensifies this.

Fish Shrinkage Debunked

The average good truth-twisting angler will tell you the fish he caught at 8 A. M. must have been 30 inches long, because when he got it home at 8 P. M. and measured it the tape showed it was 24 inches overall. The alibi most frequently used by anglers caught with undersize fish by game wardens is "Well, he was legal size when I caught him."

The shrinkages in weight estimated, or related as fact, by the majority of anglers are even higher and more exaggerated.

Actual facts secured through tests made by the West Virginia Conservation Commission shows that the average trout shrinks little more than $\frac{1}{8}$ inch over a period of several days. Most of the shrinkage occurs in the first two or three hours. After that no appreciable change in length occurs.

Therefore, all fishermen who claim a quarter inch shrinkage in six, seven or eight inch trout, as an alibi, for undersize, receive short shrift from wardens, as well as courts, and those who claim $\frac{1}{2}$ to an inch shortage where the legal lengths are ten, twelve, or fourteen inches, for bass, browns, pickerel, walleyes, landlocks, etc., are equally short-sighted and even more mendacious!

Private Pickerel Persuaders

If during hot weather, pickerel seem not interested
in usual live bait methods, skittering, bait casting lures,
etc., it's time to try one of the following three methods,
not in general use by anglers.

First: Put a quarter ounce sinker about two feet
above your minnow. Have a buckshot two and a half
feet above this. Then let your heavy sinker go way
down to the bottom in an open space alongside the
weeds, by swinging minnow and sinker away from you
and toward the weeds. As soon as the quarter ounce
sinker hits the bottom keep the line taut and slanting
toward you, and let the buckshot rest on the bottom
as far away from the heavy sinker as possible. Then let
the line go slack.

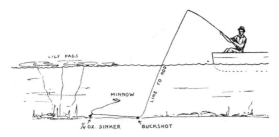

The buckshot keeps your line to the rod tip out of
the reach of the minnow which will swim up and around
to the limit of the two foot line, but can't tangle with
the rest of line held six inches beyond the two foot limit
by the buckshot.

Many times when pickerel won't bite surface and near
surface baits they'll grab the bottom fished minnow.

The same holds good for both species of bass, and
wall-eyes as well.

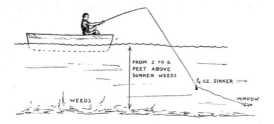

FROM 2 TO 6 FEET ABOVE SUNKEN WEEDS

¼ OZ. SINKER

MINNOW

WEEDS

Second method: Instead of playing your skitter bait of perch belly, or your streamer fly, close to the surface, allow either to sink down almost to the bottom. Play the lure in slow, short jerks along within a foot or two of the bottom, as far as you can. Then play it up, very slowly, in short jerks, to the top.

This will often produce strikes either deep in the water, or when the bait is being brought up, at times when all other methods fail.

Third method: When usual pickerel procedure is non-productive use a quarter ounce sinker to keep the minnow way down deep in the water, and slowly drift over sunken weed beds, with your bait as near the bottom as you can keep it without fouling. If there's no wind keep the boat in slow motion with the oars, or just simply still fish, as deep as possible, without tangling in weeds, but change your location ten or eleven feet every few minutes. This is often a last resort pickerel producer.

Can You Tell 'Em Apart?

The struggle ceased! A mighty fish triumphantly was boated!

"Hurrah!" I cried, "Oh what a pike!" And boastfully I gloated.

"No! No!" my friend exclaimed, "That fish, so big and strong and husky,

"Is not a pike, you greenhorn chump—that is a splendid muskie!"

The guide just slowly shook his head—his grin was pained and mournful.

"A pick'ril is a pick'ril, boys!" he said in tones most scornful!

—M. W. B.

Yellow Perch, Red Perch, White Perch, Pike-Perch, Which?

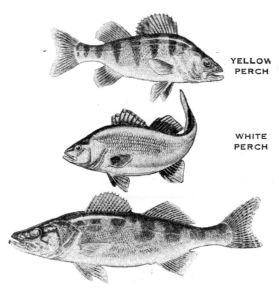

YELLOW
PERCH

WHITE
PERCH

"PIKE PERCH" OR "WALL-EYE"

The yellow perch (top) is often called "red perch," but by whichever name designated, is the same, and one of the finest of all pan-fish. It is impossible to mistake it for any other species, as its green stripes against a yellow background are its own particular pattern, not shared by any American fresh water fish.

The white perch (middle) of New England and a portion of eastern Canada, is really not a perch at all, but a sea bass, and, although found in many fresh lakes and ponds, came originally from the ocean. It is one of the worlds' finest pan-fish, many fishermen preferring it to trout for good eating. It is white and silvery, darker on the back, and often has a blue-purplish tint at the throat-latch, or V between the lower gills.

The "pike perch" (bottom) is the same fish as the "wall-eyed" pike. Both names are misleading, as it is not a pike of any kind. If anglers would simply call this fish a "wall-eye," much of the confusion which exists regarding it would be cleared up, as the word "wall-eye" doesn't describe any other American fish but this, with its prominent eyes, and their peculiar vitreous gleam—a sort of translucent moonstone effect. Although the "pike-perch" is a true perch (count its back fin spines—then count those of the yellow perch—they number the same, 13) it doesn't resemble a pike in any respect. (See picture of Great Northern pike on Page 17).

Call It Crappie or Calico?

While members of the same general family, those two popular panfishes, the Crappie and the Calico Bass, are two distinct species.

The Crappie has only five or six spines in the dorsal fin, while the Calico Bass has from seven to eight. Therefore, if you'll just remember "Six or less spines—Crappie" and "Seven or more spines—Calico," you can always tell these two fish apart.

Both these fish differ from the Sunfish ("Kivvie" or "Punkin' seed") in the fact that they are mottled, and generally much larger. The Crappie is a sort of olive-silver, mottled dark green on the upper body, with the back (dorsal) fin and the tail mottled with dull green. The Calico is much the same color with the markings darker and covering the entire body and all the fins.

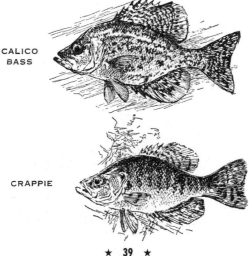

CALICO
BASS

CRAPPIE

Swashbucklers of the Sea!

Many tuna of 700 pounds and more have been landed. Deep sea anglers state that 1000 pounders are not uncommon in the ocean.

The Blue Marlin, like the Sailfish, is not a true swordfish. He belongs to the billfish family, and some exceed 500 pounds in weight.

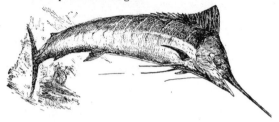

BLUE MARLIN

The Bluefish, although seldom taken weighing over 15 pounds, is one of the most savage of ocean fish, wantonly killing thousands of smaller fish it can't possibly eat.

The broadbill swordfish, noted for its endurance and the terrific fight it puts up, is a true swordfish. Quarter ton specimens are not uncommon, although few of that weight are landed each season.

The Sailfish doesn't jump with his sail spread out, as most artists, with artistic license, picture them. He rarely exceeds 100 pounds on the Atlantic Coast, but has been caught weighing 215 pounds in the Pacific.

The Tarpon, magnificent game fish though he may be, is only a large herring! He sometimes exceeds 200 pounds!

The largest Striped Bass of record, landed by commercial fishermen, weighed 112 pounds. The rod and reel record is 73 pounds.

The streamlined, gamy Amberjack has been taken weighing over 100 pounds, on rod and reel.

TUNA

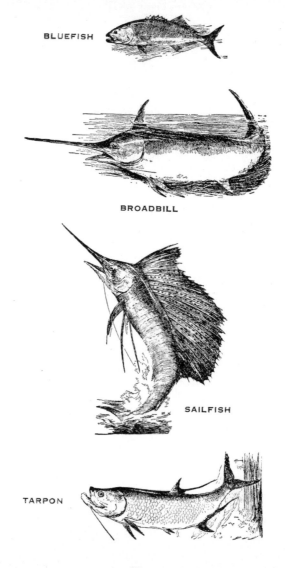

BLUEFISH

BROADBILL

SAILFISH

TARPON

STRIPED BASS

AMBERJACK

How to Ease or Escape Various Camp Discomforts

Sunburn. If you will wait till after three thirty (Daylight Saving Time) before exposing arms, legs, shoulders, etc., to the sun and wind, you'll tan, not burn. I first learned this from an aticle by Dr. Irving Cutter in the Boston Herald, and not only followed this advice myself, but persuaded several friends to try it. Result: we all escaped sunburn, and soon tanned to a point where we could take the full sun earlier and longer.

Don't make the common error of believing that you won't burn on cloudy or hazy days. You can acquire extremely painful sunburns even though the sun is behind clouds all day.

A good way to acquire a gradual tan against sunburn is to limit your first day's exposure to the brightest sunlight (10 A.M. to 2:30 P.M.) to ten minutes the first day, fifteen the second, twenty the third, twenty-five the fourth, thirty the fifth, etc.

Pale, tender skins are helped to withstand sunburn by rubbing on tannic-acid jelly, coca butter, olive oil, vinegar, or one of the trade preparations sold to minimize sunburn, but none of them will keep you from burning if your skin is exposed too long.

Any of the above preventatives will help alleviate discomfort from sunburn if applied liberally to the skin by patting. It is especially important to avoid rubbing.

Sterile gauze compresses dipped in very strong tea or Epsom Salts solution will help when other remedies are not available.

Bee and Wasp Stings: Squeeze the flesh around the puncture, to force out as much venom as possible, and cover with a bicarbonate of soda paste, or with a compress wet with ammonia, or with a mud poultice!

Mosquitos and Black Flies: An ounce of prevention is worth a pound of cure—so carry along a good anti-mosquito, anti-fly lotion. Here's a good one you can have your druggist make up, as he knows how to mix it so there'll be no free acid to burn the skin: One part carbolic acid to ten parts sweet oil, or if your skin is extraordinarily tender one part acid to twelve parts oil. There are many good commercial insect repellents, but they must be applied frequently to be effective—in bad fly country as often as every fifteen minutes. The carbolic and oil mixture is effective for longer periods.

Midges: To keep midges, "no-seeums," etc., from going through mosquito netting and screens, spray the netting two or three times a day with kerosene, Flit, Gulfspray, or other good commercial insecticide.

Chiggers or Red Bugs: Dust powdered sulphur liberally over the neck, forearms, wrists, legs, and ankles. Dust it on, and rub in, the collar, lower sleeves, socks, and lower pant legs. Kerosene applied to all these spots also keeps chiggers away, but some people's noses and skins are "allergic" to kerosene. However, an ounce of oil of bergamot to four ounces of kerosene is easier to get along with for sensitive souls!

Chiggers, which have burrowed into the skin, can be killed with a drop of ether or Energine. Hold the hand over the liquid to prevent too rapid evaporation.

Insect in the Ear: The instant an insect gets inside the ear turn it to the sun. In nine cases out of ten the offender will crawl out. In the tenth case a few drops of glycerine or sweet oil will kill or expel the intruder. If the insect dies and remains in the ear after the above treatment, fill the ear with warm water, which will float out the oil and the insect.

Here's a Good Insect "Driver-off-er"

　　　½ oz. oil of citronella
　　　½ oz. oil of cedar
　　　¼ oz. pennyroyal oil
　　　¼ oz. spirits of camphor
　　2½ oz. white petroleum
　　1　 oz. pine tar

You can leave out the pine tar, but it helps retain the potency of the preparation.

Are Beavers Web-Footed?

Yes and no. The hind feet, used in swimming, are webbed, but the front feet are not.

Salty Secrets for Sea Anglers

Tips, Tricks, "Takers"

As there is a vast army of fresh water anglers whose interest in sea game fishing awakens actively each year, but to whom the subject is a total or comparative mystery, we believe it within the scope of this book to unveil information enough to teach these tyros the essentials of taking salt water gamesters.

On the whole, as sea game fish are bigger, heavier, stronger, and speedier than fresh water fish, hooks must be huskier, lines longer, and reels and rods more robust.

Fresh water hooks ordinarily used increase in size from No. 16 to No. 1, and where they stop in size, the hooks generally used in salt water begin, and grow larger, starting with 1/0, which is a size larger than No. 1, and ending up with 16/0, which is husky enough to hold a half ton or more of sea-monster!

Although many braided lines of cotton, linen, silk and Nylon are used in sea fishing the great, great majority of sea anglers prefer "cuttyhunks," of twisted linen. Cuttyhunks are classified by the number of threads twisted together into one line, varying from 6 to 72, and test from two to three pounds per thread breaking strength when wet. Thus even the smallest 6 thread sea line of fine quality tests 18 pounds, as compared to fine "spinning" lines for fresh water testing only four or five pounds.

SALT WATER HOOKS (TOP)
COMPARED TO
FRESH WATER HOOKS (BOTTOM
SHOWING ACTUAL SIZES

Ocean reels, like ocean hooks, range from 1/0, the smallest to 16/0 the largest, in general use. The "0" is said to stand for "ocean," in both hook and reel classifications. The smallest of ocean reels holds at least 200 yards of 9 thread (27 lbs. test) line, and capacity increases rapidly, so that a 4/0 holds 500 yards, and a 6/0 some 700 yards of 9 thread Cuttyhunk.

When you get up into the stronger, and larger lines, you'll need larger reels. For instance, the same 4/0 that holds 500 yards of 9 thread, will hold only 300 yards of 18 thread, and the 6/0 that takes 700 yards of 9 thread will take only 390 yards of 24 thread line. You'll need a husky 12/0 for 400 yards of 36 thread line, and when you get into 54 threads you'll need the very largest standard size reels, from which you can graduate into still larger made-to-order reels holding over a half mile of 172 lb. test line!

BIG SEA GAME FISH HOOKS
(NEEDLE EYES)

In most standard salt water rods only the tips are weighed, and vary from 2 to 45 ounces, the butts being detachable. However, many salt water, like fresh water, rods are made all in one piece.

Leaders are generally steel piano wire, or stainless steel "cable." Wire leaders are usually #6, #8, or #10, and go up to #16 for giant blue-fins, etc.

You can get a complete serviceable outfit from around ten dollars for bay fishing, to almost anything you want to pay for broadbill or bluefin tackle, which runs into real money, as it must be built throughout to stand terrific punishment.

WHAT OUTFIT?

The best all-round outfit for the beginner, who may encounter conditions where he would like to do practical fishing of several different kinds, is a boat-rod, free-spool reel with star drag, and an 18 thread Cuttyhunk. With this tackle you can do most bay, inlet, wharf, jetty, and general "inside" still and drift fishing, as well as light, and medium heavy trolling along outer beaches and reefs, and almost all channel and pass fishing; in short, all types where you expect fish from two or three up to about 60 pounds. Besides these, you can use this combination for effective surf casting both out through the breakers, and in towards the rocks from a boat.

A very serviceable, dependable, and efficient outfit for this all-round fishing is:

Reel: "Quadruple multiplying," capacity 200 yards 18 thread Cuttyhunk, star drag, free spool, "throw-off," easy to oil, leather thumb drag. Cost, approximately $8.50.

Line: 200 yards 15 thread untreated Cuttyhunk, testing 45 lbs. Cost, approximately $3.00.

Leader: 3 feet of #6 piano wire, or small size cable wire, with snap, or "split link," #4 swivel. Cost, approximately 50c.

Rod: Short butt boat rod type, butt from 18 to 20 inches long, with a 5 to 6 foot tip of 5 to 7 oz. weight. Material, split bamboo with wood butt, or all steel. Guides and top stainless steel, chrome or agate. It is important not to select a rod with too long a butt. This is the secret of comfort in boat fishing, as you don't want your reel way off where it's a strain to reach it when playing fish. Cost, approximately $8.00. Total cost, $20.

FOR SURF-CASTING

While you can do good practical surf fishing with the all-round outfit described on Page 20, and can learn the essentials with it, for really expert work, and greater pleasure, you'll come eventually to a real surf-rod, and a lighter line, and perhaps as you get more expert change over to a reel without a drag.

However, as an inexperienced caster, you'll do better in landing fish to stick to the same reel we advised for your all-round tackle. But, as you progress, you'll begin to want more leverage, and greater power on the cast, in your rod, and greater flexibility, and less wind resistance in your line.

If you expect to do much surf-casting, therefore, or surf-casting exclusively, it would be best to start out with the most efficient rod, with a split bamboo tip from 6½ to 7½ feet long, weighing 14 to 16 ounces, and a wooden butt 28 to 30 inches long, weighing from approximately 15 to about 18 ounces. The reel-seat should be locking, the guides agate, agatine, or corrodeless steel.

The line should be 12 thread, and, as you get fairly expert, a nine threader casts even easier, and further with less effort.

You'll also need a leather surf butt rest, costing about $1.50, and a galvanized sand-spike to hold your rod and reel up out of the sand when you relinquish the rod for any reason—price about $1.00.

SECRETS OF SURF-CASTING SUCCESS

Wet your line before you cast. Pour water over it. You won't have half so many back-lashes.

Cast when the breaker is coming up, so that artificial or natural bait falls into the white water and gets more and natural action.

Play fish easily—you've got all the time there is—and that's a lot! You'll not only have more fun, but you'll while away many moments which would otherwise be idle, if you make the play long drawn out—not to mention saving many a big fish you could easily lose through too much haste.

Keep the line tight—guard against slack when the fish is in the break or when the wash tosses him toward you.

Usually a rising tide, from ninety minutes on, after the turn, up to full flood, is most productive, although the ebb, from flood to half-tide, is often as good, especially the two hours after the turn.

Watch for edges of reefs, bars, sluices, gullies, and run outs. Spot these at dead low tide, write down in a note book, and you'll know where the tide will wash through on both its rise and fall. These spots are where you'll find the most of the feeding fish. The sloughs and pockets are rich pastures for hungry gamesters.

If the water becomes cloudy, dirty, full of seaweed, move on to a clear spot, if you can find one.

Watch the gulls and terns. If gulls stay around, and sit tight on the water, better stick around yourself, for there's usually bait, and bigger fish after it, in them there waters! If the terns are busy diving through the air after bait fish you'll know that game fish aren't far away!

MORE SURF-FISHING TIPS

Don't cast clear across the ocean! Twenty to sixty yards is enough—and twenty yards, with the lure over slough or wash or gully is better than sixty no-where-in-particular.

Easy does it! Timing, co-ordination, reliance on rod leverage, rather than brute strength, make for easier, more accurate casting.

Get an experienced surf-caster to show you how to make a "fish-finder" rig, or buy one.

A snap swivel, or split-link swivel, on the end of your leader, saves a lot of time changing hooks, lures, and baits.

Short, water-repellent pants, worn outside your rubber boots, keep the water from curling into your boot tops.

Try a smaller casting squid if a large one doesn't stir 'em up! And if it has become lack lustre, scrape it into brightness with your knife edge.

Save nasty wounds, eyes, ears, scalps, etc., of spectators and fishing partners by a backward glance every time before you cast! Three ounce lead sinkers or 6/0 hooks are bad medicine for too close on-lookers!

Keep a carborundum stone in your kit—not the usual hook-hone but a stone with which you can whet your knife as well as keep hooks keen pointed.

Rinse your Cuttyhunk line in fresh water after fishing —especially if it has been in weeds and dirty, sand-filled water. It will last months longer.

Put a piece of pork rind, chamois, or rag (in a pinch) on the hook of your casting squid, to add to its luring quality. And reel it in *fast*—just about as fast as you can!

BIG SEA-GAME FISH

We will not go into the details of angling for heavy sea-game fish, as that is a highly technical subject, and you'll need the advice and personal co-operation of an expert to get an adequate outfit, but in case you want to try it without purchasing an outfit, you'll find many charter boats with complete outfits, and experienced skippers ready and willing to tell you how to fish. Therefore, confining this article to light, medium, and medium heavy fishing, here are a few secrets both of the "old-timers" and the most modern anglers, that will be of great help in getting more fun and better results in salt water.

SECRET OF TOPPING TROLLING RESULTS

Practically all live or cut bait when trolled should glide smoothly through the water, without revolving, darting, or erratic motion—exactly contrary to standard fresh water practice! A good way to control cut bait, minnows, or other small bait fish, is to run the hook back far enough into the bait so that only the eye shows at the head end. A short piece of fine wire can then be run through the bait, or sewed through the lips of the minnow, and then through the hook-eye, and clinched up around the leader. If you want to take a little longer, and do a more thorough job, you can sew the bait on with old six thread Cuttyhunk, or old braided silk bait casting line, and wrap securely above the eye of the leader after threading through the hook-eye.

Another wrinkle: if bait still turns, wrap another fine wire closely around the gills, and force the ends into the flesh, to hold in place. Or sew the gills down tight with thread.

Another "kink": if you are getting bait stripped off without hooking fish, use a long shank hook, let it project way down near tail, and then sew on or wire on as directed above.

WILD TURKEYS are the fastest flying American upland game birds. Turkeys can hit a speed of 55 miles an hour.

"STRIPER-GETTER"

With a sea-worm on a three hook tandem and with a nine-foot gut leader troll slowly. If no strikes after twenty minutes or so, bend on a small sinker just ahead of the leader. If Stripers won't take this, after twenty minutes trial, bend on another sinker, and so on, till your bait is down deep enough to hit fish "where they are."

RINSE 'EM AND RETAIN 'EM!

Steel rods of all kinds should be thoroughly rinsed in fresh water, then dried thoroughly, then wiped with an oil-soaked rag, after every trip. Many anglers also wipe them again thoroughly with the oily rag before setting out.

Silk fly and bait casting lines need thorough fresh water rinsing after each trip. Then dry them out in a shady place.

These treatments add years to the rod's life, months to the line's!

FERRULE'S STUCK?

If you can't separate the joints of your rod due to tightly stuck ferrules, hold a lighted match under the outside ferrule and revolve it. Then quickly, while the outside ferrule is expanded, unjoint the rod. If you occasionally wipe the male ferrule thoroughly with a rag lightly saturated with light reel oil, and also wipe out the female ferrule with the same rag, tightly twisted, you'll avoid much ferrule trouble.

Another way to unjoint tight ferrules is to hold the rod behind you, with the ferrule behind and between the knees. Now squat, gripping each section with the knees and hands just outside the knees. Then spread the knees apart. This ought to do the trick.

TROLLING SPEED

Go faster for mackerel and blues than for stripers and pollock, generally, although if pollock won't hit slowly trolled bait they will often wake up when you put on more speed!

On the whole, a good rule is: more speed near the surface, slower when well down.

KINKS TO END ALL KINKS!

Use the ordinary keel sinker, which has the bulk of the weight below the line, pinched on the line just ahead of the swivel, to avoid twisting or untwisting the line.

Or—tie a dipsy sinker to the forward eye of the swivel, letting the dipsy hang down below the line.

Or—use two swivels, with a connecting link between them, to which you have fastened a dipsy sinker.

Or—use an ordinary tin or aluminum "trolling fin" or "rudder," which hangs down like a keel from the line ahead of the leader, and offers too much resistance flatwise against the water to be turned over by the revolving lure.

Or—use a triangle of brass or galvanized wire, with a swivel at each corner of the base, one for the leader, one for the line, and a sinker tied or snapped to the apex corner, which hangs down below line and leader.

Or—make a simple "U" bend in heavy galvanized wire, and put a small closed loop in each end. Tie a piece of line across the top of the "U" to keep it from opening up under the strain of a fighting fish. Wrap on some sheet lead, or wrap on with wire a small bolt, at the bottom of the "U." Tie the line to one closed loop of the wire, the leader to the other.

Swivels can be kept from corroding by keeping them in a wide-mouthed bottle of oil, with a hooked wire standing in the oil to use for fishing 'em out.

WHAT BAIT?

The old-timer really knows what fish are feeding on by cutting open the first one caught and examining the stomach contents.

On the whole, artificial lures which seem closest to natural foods, are the sea anglers chief dependences, where natural bait isn't used. Feather jigs, which look like squid, are leading producers all over the world. And the bright squids which have the silvery color of sand eels, menhaden, herring, sperling, and mullet are stand-bys everywhere.

If "attractors," like spinners, are used with bait, often a double spinner does a better job than a single blade. Used with sea-worms double spinners are deadly on stripers and pollock.

Fresh or frozen squid are the old-timer's reliance. Use the head, a two inch piece of the body, or the whole squid for big bass. Or cut a pennant shaped piece, peeling off the skin, and thus making the bait white and more visible. The head alone is easier to cast when surf-fishing.

Baits good for both trolling and surf are 4 or 5 inch herring, sea worms, cut mackerel or herring, small eels, eel skin lures, etc.

Most exciting way to take mackerel is with a fly-rod, and bucktail flies, or with one of those fly-rod wobbling spoons (red and white). A six inch fine wire leader, ahead of lure or fly, keeps them from being bitten off.

To catch green crabs for bait tie a couple of aging fish heads on a piece of tarred line and anchor to a rock or stake in shallow water. If you set several of these along the shore line fifteen or twenty yards apart and keep working them all you'll soon get all the bait you need.

Cut the larger ones in half from front to back and hook through between the tough part in between the legs.

Fiddler crabs can be pried out of their holes in the grass with a sharp stick, or when on the sand or mud, can be herded into the "V" of a miniature snow-plow-like arrangement of boards you drop in front of a batch of them as they scurry off·for the nearby grass.

Secrets of Forecasting Weather

Fishermen, keep your weather-eye on the clouds! That's the Number One local weather sharp's first secret.

If the clouds have a thick wooly appearance, with dome-like tops, and fairly horizontal bases, and they appear soft and fleecy, there's little prospect of any immediate disturbance. But when these cumulus clouds begin to change, and their bellies expand and grow dark, it's time to sit up and take notice. Watch the cloud wall behind them carefully. If that is darkening, gray, and ominous, watch out for thunderstorms and squalls.

Almost everybody knows and recognizes the familiar "thunder-heads." Dome-shaped, or global, they look bloated and threatening, and are much darker, usually lower hanging. They appear restless and forbidding. Usually they are accompanied by stringy sheets, and they mean "Storm coming immediately, if not sooner!"

WHEN THE SUN AT DAWN BREAKS ABOVE THE CLOUDS (A HIGH DAWN) LOOK FOR GOOD SALMON AND WALL-EYE WEATHER

On the whole a red sky, or a brilliant sunset at night, betoken fair weather next morning, but a coppery or yellow sky usually indicates a disturbance before morning, rain, or wind, or both. On the other hand a red morning sun indicates coming rain.

WHEN THE SUN AT DAWN BREAKS ABOVE THE HORIZON, LOOK FOR A NICE DAY WITH LESSENING WIND.

Look for good salmon or wall-eye weather following a "high-dawn," when the first daylight breaks above a bank of clouds. This forecasts a windy day.

When the first signs of dawn light up low on the horizon, the weather promises to be fair, with lessening wind.

Almost as reliable as the signs of an approaching thunder-storm are those indications of a coming change in the weather, high wisps, or curling clouds, followed by patches of furrowed clouds, or cloud mottled areas. These generally portend a change within 24 hours.

Like "thunder-heads," wind clouds generally betoken quick action. Therefore, when you see dark, angry looking clouds, with ragged areas, which look wind-tossed and buffeted about, watch out for an immediate blow.

If you discover a high layer of clouds passing the sun, or some far landmark like a mountain, in a different direction than the lower lying clouds, or in a different direction than the wind where you are, this forecasts a freshening wind, and often a shift in the wind's direction, generally from the direction where the high clouds are.

Speaking of wind, when a rain squall or thunder-storm is preceded by wind look for a calm when the rain is over.

"When wind precedes a sudden shower,
    Look for quiet weather in an hour!"

But when the wind starts up after the rain is falling, you can expect continuing and increasing winds.

"When wind begins while it is raining,
    Look for wind to keep on gaining."

The amateur weather forecaster will do well to consult some of the old-timers about one particular thing which is very important in estimating whether rain will stop, or continue, etc. That is, what direction does the local "good weather come from."

For instance, at most spots on the Atlantic Seaboard clearing weather normally comes from the West, when the wind is West. Mountains, prevailing air currents, prairies, etc., often affect local conditions. It is, therefore, wise to ask the experienced guides, captains, and expert amateurs, about local ruling weather conditions, if you are in a strange locality.

Shifting winds in the middle latitudes, where prevailing winds usually are from the West, usually announce a change in the weather. A shift to wind from the East generally presages a storm; to the south, rain; to the northeast colder and rain, snow or sleet; to the northwest, cooler, dryer weather.

When smaller stars disappear, and the big ones shine only dimly, you can look for rain tomorrow.

"A ring around the moon
  Means rain is coming soon"—

is a true weather-proverb, as the ring wouldn't be there unless the air contained moisture. The smaller this ring is the quicker you can look for rain, because a decreasing corona means moisture-drops increasing in size.

With halos of light in clouds, however, the opposite is true—the small halos mean slow-coming rain, the large ones indicate that it will arrive more quickly.

Hunter's Prayer

Lord, when sunset's golden glory floods across the western hills,
And the sigh of dying breezes lulls to rest upon the rills—
When the wrinkle of the ripples disappears from mirrored streams,
And the lakes lie still and placid where reflected purple gleams—
When the graying shadows lengthen, and the dark'ning dusk grows deep,
As the drowsy leaves' low rustle stills the sleepy bird's last cheep—
When the flame of larking campfires flares and flickers through the night—
When the tiny trembling stars above are twinkling points of light—
When the fragrant smoke of pipes alight goes wreathing on the breeze,
And the hunters' voices ring with song and chorus through the trees—
Lord, at last let slumber sift upon each hunter's magic dreams—
Lord, in sleep let setters point and pheasant flush beside the streams!
Lord, in sleep let cracking singles roar, and doubles echo, too!
And then with tomorrow's waking, Lord, make all these dreams come true!

—M. W. B.

Secrets of Successful Rubber-Saving

First, dry out your waders, boots, and garments after using. Perspiration allowed to remain and dry slowly in boots, waders, and waterproof clothing, is their surest and most powerful destroyer. If you don't want to take the trouble of rinsing out in tepid fresh water, as many of my friends do before arranging the article to dry, be sure to adopt immediate and adequate methods of drying.

To Dry Boots

When you have nothing else available roll up a news-paper and stick it perpendicularly in the legs of boots which have been drawn down to the knee on the out-side. One paper is better than a thick roll, as this allows more air to circulate.

The next best drying help is a "boot-board," of heavy cardboard, wall-board, or plywood, cut to fit the boot leg's inside. Slide this down into the boot at right angles to the toe. My own private boot-board has a big wedge cut out of the bottom to allow free air circulation when resting on the bottom of the boot.

The general plan of the boot-board is like Figure A.

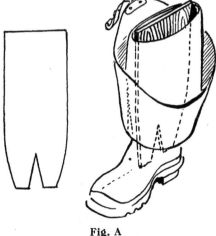

Fig. A

When this has been properly inserted, and the boots are stood up with one side close enough to the fire to warm it but not heat it too hot, the warm air on that side rises and induces colder air to flow in on the opposite side of the board. While the boot will dry out even without heat on one side, this method certainly speeds the process.

Caution: Don't set boots too close to fire or radiator.

After boots are thoroughly dry don't stand them up where they'll wrinkle, or the folds will "set." Hang them up full length by the feet. And do the same with waders, if they have boot-feet. If waders have soft feet you'll have to hang them by the waist, but be sure they're high enough on the hook so they stretch out full length and have no wrinkles or folds.

To hang up boots or waders by the feet is easier said than done. This writer uses two methods.

First, as shown in sketch #1, I tie together the ends of a six foot length of strong cord, or heavy cuttyhunk line. Then stuff the boot or wader foot fairly snugly with about three double pages of newspaper. Throw a double loop around the ankle as shown at A. Then cross the cord and throw two loops around the instep as at B. Pass the bight C of the cord under these two loops, and draw tight. Hang by C.

Fig. 1

MOOSE MORONS. By concensus American hunters of big game vote the moose top honors for bone-headedness. He will hide his head behind a bush and think he is all concealed. He is easily deceived by alleged "moose calls," and although every hunter uses a different sounding call any male within hearing answers it.

Or you can take an ordinary pair of wire coat hangers, cut each wire about 5 inches from where they come together and bend in the ends as shown in the illustration Fig. 2.

Hook under the extension projecting from the sole and hang up as shown. The boot will hang quite securely.

METAL HANGER

Fig. 2

How to Dry Waders

To dry boot-foot waders thoroughly hang up by the feet in a warm dry place and turn the waist up as high as the crotch. Tighten the draw string to keep in position.

To dry stocking foot waders turn them inside out to a few inches above the feet. (Avoid turning the feet inside out, as this puts undue strain, friction, and folds in the fabric.)

Hang upside down with four ordinary spring clip clothes pins through which you have inserted cord through the hollow spring. Cord can be attached to closet hooks, or clothes-line reel at the necessary angles to keep waders open to the air. Turn back the waist to the crotch and hold in position by tightening draw cord.

As soon as waders are dry, turn right side out, straighten and hang by waistband in closet, till needed.

In drying waders I always make the folds, just above the feet and at the crotch, at a different point every time. This avoids folding at one point so much that it weakens the fabric, the coating, or waterproof filling there.

Here's a Rubber Saver

Although rinsing in plain tepid or cold water, before drying out, helps eliminate perspiration-rot in waders, rubber garments and boots, you can do much to keep them longer, and in better condition, if you follow this prescription: First wash boots or rubber waders with pure mild soap-suds (not laundry soap but Ivory, Fairy, Swan, etc.). Then rinse.

Wader Wisdom

Check your waders for leaks before the season opens, and, if used often, perhaps once or twice during the season, by filling with water to a point just below the crotch. The water's too heavy and strains them badly if you fill way up to the brim. In a direct light look for damp spots or drops of water showing on the surface. Mark these spots, if there are any, with a circle.

To test the upper portion empty out the water in the legs and tie each leg tightly at the crotch with a strong strip of cloth, so no water can get into the legs. Then fill the upper wader with water, and mark damp spots and drops with a circle. Cloth is used in place of cord to tie legs as cord can cut the fabric if drawn too tight.

This isn't as easy as it sounds. You will have to pin the back part of the waders to the waist of the waders to a strong clothesline with as many clothespins as possible after doubling the upper inch and a half of the waist back over the line. Do the same to the front part of the waist on another clothesline strung parallel to the first about four inches from it.

All this support is necessary, as the heavy weight of the water will otherwise sag the waistline, spill water, and throw your leak locating all off.

When the waders have been turned inside out and dried thoroughly they will be easy to patch at the circled spots, if too many and too big leaks haven't put in an appearance. If leaks look pretty bad better send the waders to the Hodgman Repair Service, where they can be fixed up a lot bettter than you can do it.

The places where leaks occur oftenest are those spots which, in spite of reinforcement, give way due to taking by far the most punishment.

Watch These Points

Don't buy waders with the feet so small you can't comfortably wear heavy wool sox in them. Too tight a fit in the feet strains and starts seams, produces worn areas where the fabric is taut. On the other hand, too loose a fit causes wrinkles, which also rub through.

Sand, grit, and tiny sharp stones which work between waders and wading socks cause abrasions and leaks. Strong rubber bands sewn into the tops of these socks will hold them tight against the wader ankle and exclude most of this damaging sand and grit.

With boot-foot waders this leak factor is entirely eliminated, as, of course, there is no opportunity for chafing or abrasion.

Don't walk long distances from your home or camp in your waders to reach the fishing grounds. You'll do a lot to conserve these now precious fishing togs if you wear your shoes for the long walks, waiting till you're actually at the stream before you don the waders. The shoes can be hidden and left till you return, or you can hang them over your shoulder on a sling.

Don't roll up air mattresses for storing. Inflate partially and lay flat.

And—very important, indeed, for all rubber equipment—keep grease of all kinds away from it. Wash off all grease accidentally left on rubber goods with good mild soap.

Wader and Boot Repairs

Hodgman makes a special Zephyrweight Repair Kit No. 310 for their waders Nos. 302, 305, and 325. The Hodgman Wadwell Repair Kit No. 310 is for waders Nos. 301 and 304.

These are for emergencies, "on the spot" repairs of hook holes, barb-wire perforations, cat-briar punchthroughs, etc. Heavier damage than this should be expertly and permanently taken care of in the Hodgman Repair Shop.

Repairs to waders and boots should be made immediately, for a small repair made on the spot often saves making a serious one later.

Complete directions are included in the Hodgman Repair Kits.

In case you get caught far from a Hodgman dealer, or some one has borrowed your Hodgman Repair Kit, you can make serviceable mends with the ordinary inner tube tire repair outfits.

For mending rubber boots and rubber wader feet, cleanse the area around the leak with fine emery paper or sandpaper, or if none is available, scrape it gently by rubbing your knife edge over it, back and forth, till you can see the surface is considerably dulled. Then apply a coat of rubber cement. Let it dry for several minutes, then apply a second coat, which you can smooth down evenly with a knife blade. Keep your fingers and palms off this cemented area, if you want it to hold like grim death. Now put on the rubber patch, taking care to keep fingers off its sensitized or cementized side. Apply and press down evenly, in every part. If at home, put a cold flat-iron on it and leave on a smooth, level surface, for a few hours.

In repairing the cloth covered parts of waders don't scrape or use abrasive paper very much. Just a light "dusting off," then blow away every grain of grit and lint. A quick wiping off with alcohol, if you have it, helps here. When thoroughly evaporated, treat the spot to be repaired with a coat of cement (plenty), allow to dry before the next coat is applied, and press on the patch as described above.

A piece of board, or flat metal, pressed on the patch by a heavy stone, and left there for several minutes helps make a lasting repair that won't roll back at one or two corners, or on the side.

Rubber mattresses can be repaired in the same manner, for all ordinary leaks or punctures.

Additional Repair Pointers

If you will take the pains to make patches on *both sides* (inside and out) of a tear or hole, the job will be more thorough, and almost invariably last as long as the article itself does!

If you want an almost invisible mend for a leak or puncture in an air mattress, proceed as follows: Work into the hole some rubber cement with a toothpick. Don't slop it around, use just enough. Push a half-inch piece of ordinary size rubber band (not the big flat one, just the small square one) into the hole, leaving about ⅛ inch sticking out. If the hole is not filled by one piece of band you may need one or two more. When the cement dries at this spot, shave off the protruding end of the band with an old razor blade or very sharp knife. Dust some talc or soapstone on the mended place to keep objects coming in contact with it from sticking.

And here's the secret of not only comfort in sleeping on your air mattress, but longer life for that handy adjunct to camp luxury: "don't inflate it too much."

Most beginners make the mistake of blowing up the inflatable mattress too taut. Put just enough air into it so that, when you turn sidewise, your hip will nearly, but not quite, touch the ground. With this amount of pressure you'll sleep as though buoyed up by down!

THE PORPOISE CAN OUTSWIM and outlast many of the speediest fish, and can actually swim circles about a fast steamship. When pursuing fish they select one victim in a school and follow him till, exhausted, he has to fall behind and act as dinner for the determined porpoise.

It's Not Leakage,
It's Condensation

Many wader fishermen get the idea that because they are soaking wet after a few hours fishing, that their waders leak like a sieve. Then, no matter how they look for abrasions, pin holes or snags, they can't find them and quickly decide that the waders are no good. In most cases the wetness inside the waders is caused by condensation of moisture and not through any leaks. You can prove this very quickly by hanging up the waders, filling them full of water and watching to see if any leaks out. (This is how all Hodgman waders are tested before they leave the factory.) After all, if the water leaks out, it will also leak in and in that case, there is something wrong with the waders. However, if no water leaks out and you still get wet inside the waders after a few hours fishing, then you know it is something else that is causing this moisture. Here's the explanation: Let's look at an ordinary pitcher of ice water on a warm day. After a few minutes, the outside of the pitcher is covered with moisture, it being condensation from the atmosphere which is warmer than the ice water in the pitcher. This is exactly the same phenomenon which causes rain to fall. Now, let's put on a pair of waders. Our bodies are almost 100 degrees

Fahrenheit. Therefore, inside the waders, it's going to be at least 80 degrees. Now step into water of say about 45 degrees and exactly the same thing happens that happened to the pitcher of ice water—only this time the river is the water, the waders are the pitcher and you are the warm atmosphere. Thus you are going to get wet and it's your own perspiration and not the river that is doing it. Moral: don't blame the waders unless you can find the hole.

Nifty Novelties in Knots

(Hitches That Really Hold!)

Fig. 1

Fig. 1. A simple knot like this decreases leader or line strength 50%, so keep 'em out of yours!

Fig. 2. Better far to break leader or line at the knot and tie it together with the variation of the double blood knot shown in figure 2, which has been proven stronger by textile breaking strength gauges than the usual double blood knot. Note that both ends, in this variation, project from the same side, not opposite sides, of the middle twist, as in the old double blood knot.

Fig. 2

This variation is by far the best of all knots for tieing lengths of gut or nylon together for leaders.

Fig. 3

Fig. 3. This is a variation of the "return" knot which has proven more dependable for the writer than the usual version. Wrap the leader around the hook three times, as shown, then on the final wrap-around include both shank and the main leader strand, and return the end back through all the loops. The three wraps make this knot absolutely non-slipable, even with such a tricky substance as so-called "Jap" or "Scosiatic" artificial gut. Nylon behaves marvelously in this knot.

Fig. 4

Fig. 4. We give you here a much more symmetrical and easier-to-tie knot than any "return" knot ever invented. Thread the leader through the hook-eye then double in back in a loop alongside the shaft, take three turns back along the shaft around the shank and the loop both, and on the final turn thrust the loose end through the loop. Pull on both this loose end and the main end till everything is tightened up, and then pull up snug against the eye. Not only a pretty, but a solidly dependable hitch! You can't beat it! Yet not one angler in ten thousand knows it and ties it!

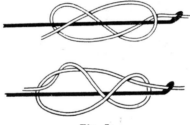

Fig. 5

Fig. 5. Here's a knot my grandfather taught me many years ago. It holds better, and is stronger, without direct cross-draw, than the "figure 8," which it somewhat resembles, as shown by the "figure 8" knot shown above it. Both knots are in position ready to tighten, below the eye of the hook, but, on flies, can be tied above the eye, which is then slipped through, and the knot tightened.

COYOTES CAN RUN about 40 miles per hour at top speed—5 miles per hour slower than Jack-Rabbits—but they can keep this 40 miles speed longer than the Jacks can maintain their 45 mile rate!

The Wizardry of Weight
and
Legerdemain of Length

(Secrets of Knowing Actual Weights, Heights, Etc., Without Instruments)

Height by Shadow

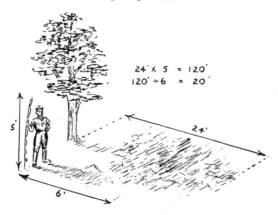

$$24' \times 5 = 120'$$
$$120' \div 6 = 20'$$

To measure the height of a cliff, tall tree, building, etc., which casts a shadow, measure your own shadow and then the shadow of the object. Multiply the length of the object's shadow by that of your own height, and then divide the result by the length of your own shadow. This will give the height of the object.

Fish Weight by Balanced Pole

Balance a pole on the upper edge of a double bitted axe driven into the top of a stump, or on a piece of rock, with a sharp edge uppermost, placed on a stone wall, flat boulder, or stump. If the pole tapers, add weight (say sinkers tied to a line fastened to the end of the pole) till the balance point is exactly half way between the ends of the pole. Then hang any known weight (a two or four pound carton of sugar, say) to one end of the pole, and the fish to be weighed to the other. Move the pole to a point where it will again balance, and measure the respective distances to each end from the point of balance. Multiply the known weight by its distance in inches from the balance point, and divide by the distance in inches of the fish from the balance point. This will give a mighty close approximation, very close, indeed, to the fish's actual weight. The formula is: "The known weight, multiplied by its distance from the point of balance is equal to the product of the unknown weight and its distance from the point of balance."

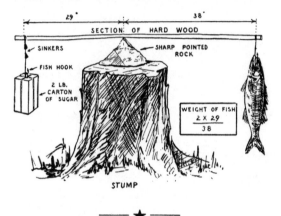

— ★ —

A Watch for A Compass

Hold the timepiece flat, so the sun shines on the face. Turn it around till the hour hand points at the sun. Be careful not to move the watch while placing the edge of a piece of paper, or a pencil across the face, resting on the dial center, and pointing half way between the figure XII or 12 and the hour hand. The line of the pencil will be approximately north and south, in the northern hemisphere only. While helpful, this is a long way from being as accurate as a good compass, however!

— ★ —

VALLEY QUAIL CHICKS can run for cover, if frightened, immediately after hatching, and with parts of the shell still clinging to their backs!

Identifying the Tracks

SEE ACCOMPANYING CHART

1. Black bear, left hind foot
2. Grizzly bear, left front foot
3. Bighorn sheep
4. Pronghorn antelope
5. Fox
6. Canada lynx
7. Woodchuck, left hind foot
8. Mountain goat
9. Raccoon, left fore foot
10. Opossum, left fore foot
11. Elk
12. Coyote
13. Running moose
14. Running whitetail deer
15. Opossum, right hind foot
16. Bobcat
17. Running caribou
18. Black bear, left fore foot
19. Raccoon, left hind foot
20. Gray wolf
21. Moose, walking
22. Cougar
23. Grizzly, right hind foot
24. Whitetail deer, walking
25. Caribou, walking

Most of the tracks (sketches from Hunting & Fishing) on the opposite page show the prints made by the animal while walking. It is difficult to show the running tracks, except in some few cases, as the speeds vary so much in the same animal.

In practically all cases of animals with the split hoof, the marks when running are fairly similar to those of the walking animal, except that when running the spread is wider. A quick glance at the tracks pictured here will show the veriest tyro that #13, #14, #17, are tracks of running animals. Note how much closer the two halves of the hoofs are in the corresponding prints of the moose walking (#21), the whitetail deer walking (#24), and the caribou walking (#25).

Of all tracks made by game animals of America, that of the black bear's hind foot most resembles the human foot print. There is a lesser resemblance to human tracks in the prints of the grizzly's hind feet. Bears walk, trot, pace, or gallop, at will. Big horn sheep leave footprints that are blunt toed, rather than sharp. The outer edge of their hoofs make sharper impressions than the inner.

Note that in the tracks of the fox (#5), the coyote (#12) and the grey wolf (#20), the characteristic imprint of the four toes and ball of the foot, although the extremely light tread of the fox doesn't show these as plainly.

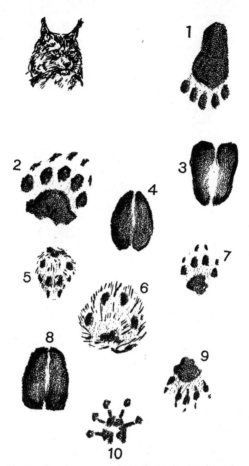

The tracks of moose and elk show the fact that these two are among the slower big game animals. The moose in flight runs with an action exactly like that of a trotting horse (the resemblance is startling if you watch the legs and feet only), and rarely can do faster than 28 miles an hour. The elk will gallop, when hard pressed, but naturally trots when in a hurry. Elks are slightly faster. A young bull or cow might do 30 miles an hour for short distances only. The trim, compact

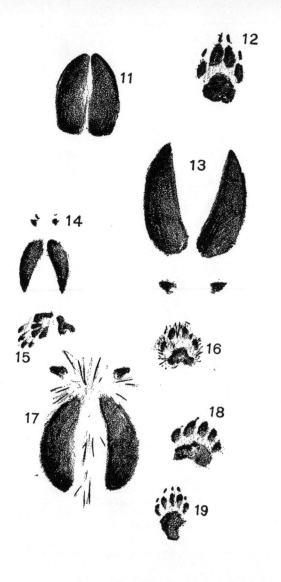

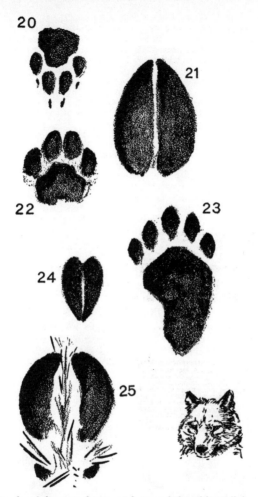

tracks of the pronghorn antelope and the white tail deer are indicative of greater speed. The prong horn, fastest of all American game can hold a robust 40 miles per hour for long stretches!

While the white tail can do as fast as 45 to 47 miles per hour in short bursts when running for it's life, it holds to about 35 miles in longer stretches! However, as the white tail lives mostly in thick cover, speed isn't so important to him as his tremendous jumping power, enabling him to leap over dead timber, etc., which his pursuers have to go around. A walking white tail keeps his toes together, the hind foot steps into the fore foot. On the other hand, the running white tail leaves the plain imprint of four hoofs at each jump in his galloping run. From front track to back will be about four feet for each gallop.

Young deer make smaller tracks. Does make lighter tracks, usually, than bucks—but the novice can be greatly confused in trying to decide what sex and age made lone individual tracks, as a heavy doe will make deeper tracks than a young spike-horn.

The caribou leaves a four toed track, whether running or walking, with the dew claws making the smaller print back of the toes, and all his footprints are widely spread, as his feet are adapted to walking on snow and ice. These dew claws in white tail deer, show only in the snow, or soft wet ground.

Secrets of Wing Shooting For More Game!

HOW TO KILL CROWS

There are no Federal or State laws, no off season, no bag limits, on Jim Crow, that destructive game bird egg and fledgling eater! And every time you kill one of the black-hearted rascals, you get valuable wing shooting practice, and you eliminate one more game bird

KILL THE BLACK PIRATES!

destroyer, of insatiable appetite, extraordinary cunning, and gangster propensities.

It is by taking advantage of this cunning and gang spirit that you can eliminate the largest number of crows. Whenever crows are led to believe that a fellow gangster is in distress they will at once fly to the rescue.

Therefore a good crow-call, and the ability to make it sound like the wails of a beset brother and the calls of a fellow mobster for help, will bring the gang near enough to your hiding place so that you can do real execution as the black bandits mob up for action.

Get into the shadows of bushes, trees, and thickets, and you'll be less readily observed by the cunning crows—and to do this, pick out spots where your shadow is concealed by other shadows, if possible.

As advocated in other hunting articles in this booklet, we advise as much preliminary prospecting as possible, before you get right down to active shooting.

Crows have learned to suspect and fear men with guns. They are surprisingly bold and unafraid if you go afield unarmed, and you can, in one or two trips, discover a lot about the places where they congregate, and their various customs and fly-ways in any selected locality.

And, by the way, you can take advantage of their lessened fear for a weaponless man by hiding your gun under grass, etc. But don't hide it under branches, etc., if you have a companion with you—and even when you hide your gun in grass, or in shadows keep the safety on. You'll be surprised how quickly you can grasp it, bring it to your shoulder, throw off the safety, point, and fire!

Crows are curious, extraordinarily inquisitive. Two hunters with good crow calls can stage a mock crow-fight, with angry calls and name calling, that will bring all the crows within hearing on a quick trip of investigation. With practice, one hunter can change the tone and tempo of his call to make it seem like two angry crows in dispute.

Keep well hidden when you stage one of these mock battles. Kill as many crows as you can when they first put in an appearance. Then move on a mile or so, and stage another fake battle.

If you use a motor car for transportation, or a horse drawn vehicle, do your calling so far away that the crows can't see your transportation. Strange as it may seem, crows are not very suspicious of a saddle horse, particularly if you tether your steed where it can crop grass naturally.

If you are not very skillful at simulating a crow-battle, a few decoys will help, but after you learn, by trial and error, the peculiar angry tones that lure on the spectators, you can gather more crows around by calling than by motionless crow decoys.

"Roost Shooting"

If you will take time to locate the spot where crows roost at night, you can many times get more shooting than in any other possible way. During the day build your blind, so that the setting sun will be at your back. Put plenty of brush both in front of and behind where you sit, either on the edge of a 2½ foot deep fox hole you've dug, or on a convenient rock, stump, or log.

You can then stage your crow-call fight, or set up a stuffed owl, or do both, with good effect. Shoot the first advance guard, then keep motionless, continuing the calling, and taking the additional crows as they come in.

Your chances for longer continued shooting will be all the better if you pick out a day when the birds come in from the open fields with both the wind and the sun at your back. Crows almost invariably come into their roosts upwind.

Be sure you kill the first one or two crows that come in. Chances are that when the first one is out of the way, and can't alarm new arrivals, your chances will be greatly improved for getting more shots.

Clothes for Camouflage

One good thing about the preliminary "prospecting" of crow roosts, crow country, and crow fly-ways, is your opportunity to observe the cover, and, when you return bent on business, to dress so that you blend with it. You will be more successful in fall, in dead leaves, in khaki colored clothes and cap. In green leaves, in summer, wear green cap and shirt, with black pants. In winter, white is the best costume. In snow blinds, stand motionless in a white sheet, with white mittens, white cap, white muffler up over chin and mouth. The best costume for crow hunting in tamaracks is blue coveralls, blue shirt, blue cap. But don't wear any of these costumes in deer country in open season. Better do your crow hunting when the high power rifle brigade is idle!

Good crow decoys can be made by shaping a wire coat hanger into a crow silhouette and covering with black cloth.

Other good decoys are a cat in a cage, a tethered, captive crow nearby, a young crow or two in a cage, or a single adult crow alone, if you can't get young ones.

When crow shooting in snow, leave the dead birds scattered about. They excite crow curiosity.

With a shovel snow can be piled up into a perfect blind. Dig your trench like an inverted wedge, narrow at the top, wider at the bottom. Pile up the snow you dig out, ahead of you. Stick in some weeds or branches at the top for further concealment.

Throw your dead cows well ahead of the blind, down wind, so the crows coming in up wind, won't have to cross your blind to get a good look at the dead decoys.

Dead crows make better decoys if impaled and set up on heavy sharpened wires leading up perpendicularly from circular wire bases.

If you can catch a young crow alive in a crow trap, his raucous cawing for help is the best possible decoy for the adults.

It is estimated that crows destroyed 20,000,000 duck eggs and ducklings last season, compared to an approximate kill by wild fowlers of about 15,000,000 birds. The number of upland game birds this black marauder kills, in the egg, and as fledglings, is enormous. So all you can do to exterminate crows helps to conserve game birds.

HOW FAST DO FISH GROW?

The rate of growth depends on food, length of season when sunlight is available, and number of fish in the water competing for food.

In water fairly normal for food, fish and insects, the State of Wisconsin found that large mouth bass at the age of three were 8.9 inches long; at four years were 12.1 inches; at eight years were 15.4 inches. It requires from three to six summers for bass to grow the legal length of 10 inches.

Pickerel or pike average 20.3 inches at 4 years, and 28.1 inches at 8 years.

The wall-eye at 3 years is 14.2 inches long—at 4 years, 14.8 inches—and at 8 years, 20.8 inches.

DEER EAT DYNAMITE!

Deer relish dynamite because of the saltpeter it contains. They will lick it with gusto, till it's all gone. A New York State forest ranger reported 15 sticks eaten by deer. These had been hidden in the woods for a forthcoming July 4th celebration. Deer sign revealed the fact that they had been eaten by these forest dwellers.

Young Buck Deer begin to grow antlers within three or four months after birth. By winter time the budding antlers project an inch or two above the forehead. At about 18 months his first pair of antlers should be "in the velvet"—ready for stripping.

Duck Decoys

Secrets of Getting More Ducks
Within Range

Although on the whole most ducks, dippers as well as divers, will decoy to mallard patterns, the arrangement and location of decoys for dippers should be different than those for the divers.

The "puddle-duck," or dippers will come in better to a loosely spread group, scattered fairly well inshore, with four or five of the birds right along the shoreline, in only a few inches of water.

As most dippers are wary of shoreline, in circling into decoys, and especially will avoid timber, you will have more success placing your blind and your decoy spread where ducks don't have to circle over shore or woods, to light within range—a point, or an out-circling bend are ideal, therefore.

The diver ducks seem to come in best to a more complete decoy grouping, set fairly well out on the water, about 30 yards away from your blind.

If you want to decoy both kinds of ducks more effectively, you will do well to arrange one compact spread for the divers, about 30 yards out, in the deeper water, and one looser spread for the dippers, closer in.

There is much controversy among sportsmen as to just what type of decoy is the best, but when you stop to consider that black ducks, generally admitted to be the wariest of all, decoy by the thousands to the crudest of profile decoys each season, the advocates of meticulous attention to detail and coloring may well be puzzled. It is also true that the plain bag decoy, without any attempt at shaping a head or bill, will attract plenty of all kinds of ducks.

It is well, in balmy weather, a day or two following a rain or snow storm, to set out your spread in loose formation, as described above, for mallards.

In stormy weather the more compact arrangement for divers, has often proved its worth, to a great many canny wild-fowlers.

Along the Mississippi flyways the greater proportion of your ducks will be dippers—mallards, widgeon, pintails, teal.

Along the Atlantic and Pacific flyways, most of the birds will be redheads, canvasbacks, buffleheads, greater and lesser scaups, ruddy ducks, and goldeneyes.

SILHOUETTES

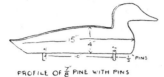

PROFILE OF $\frac{7}{8}$" PINE WITH PINS

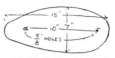

BASE BORED FOR PINS

SILHOUETTE PAINTED AND ASSEMBLED

BAG DECOYS

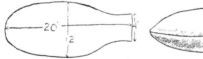

. TWO PIECES OF UNBLEACHED COTTON SEWED TOGETHER INTO A BAG

TURNED INSIDE OUT, STUFFED WITH GROUND CORK AND TIED

WITH TWO COATS OF LINSEED OIL AND TWO OF COLOR. CLOTHESPIN BILL

Unusual Decoy Tricks

1. For the diving ducks, make up and paint white, one or two decoys like seagulls. Place these near, but not among, your spread. Hunters have reported unusually good results from this trick.

★ 75 ★

2. For the dipper ducks, place a wild-goose decoy right among the ducks.

3. For canvasback, redhead, and bluebill, set up your spread in two long ragged strings, generally shaped like a V, with the point out from the shore.

If your decoys are in front or beside a point of land, which is the best of all locations, put another group in the lee, fairly close together. These "sleepers," peacefully at rest, seem to add the final, attractive, confidence-begetting touch, and the wariest flights wheel in over them.

4. If you have plenty of decoys, arrange them in two flanking groups, with a lane of open water between them. Put one or two decoys in this lane. The passing flights will often coast right into this open space!

5. One of the smartest duck hunters I ever knew arranged a couple of animated "dippers" among his decoys. Using decoys with metal bottoms for weight, he made them tip up, as though feeding, by a cuttyhunk fishing line tied to a screw eye under water at the front. This line ran straight down and through the ring of a pyramid sinker, and thence into the blind!

Most Thorough, and Easiest Way
to Pick Ducks

Melt six or seven pounds of paraffin in a deep sauce pan big enough to hold your duck. Pluck out the biggest wing feathers, and then quickly immerse the duck in the melted paraffin. As soon as well covered with paraffin, remove the duck and dip it at once into a pail or deep dishpan of cold water. Then all you have to do is pull off the congealed paraffin, bringing with it the feathers, pin-feathers, and everything. Salvage the paraffin by melting and straining out the feathers through a large fine wire strainer, or through cheese cloth.

Squirrels know where to chisel through a nutshell with the most direct results, and the least work. In the Spring they also can find, invariably, nuts buried away the preceding Fall.

How Many "Points" on Antlers?

The average adult buck, from 7 to 12 years old, has about eight points.

Swans Mate for Life

Swans are models of conjugal fidelity. They mate for life.

"Partridge Pointers"

Secrets of Successfully Finding Grouse

Whereas woodcock are worm-wanglers, and pheasant scratch-feeders, the ruffed grouse is a budder, a berrier and a fruit-eater.

FLYING RUFFED GROUSE

Grouse like timber for cover, smaller woods, buddy woods, berry patches, apple orchards, grape vines, and the like for food spots.

If, during the Spring and Summer, you'll locate wild grapes, black berry, partridge berry, wintergreen berry, poplar, cedar, and birch bud strips adjoining the bigger, taller woods, you'll be spotting some ideal "partridge" haunts for use later.

Such feeding spots located at a little distance from timber are also good resources to check up—and so are orchards near timber, or not too far away.

MALE RUFFED GROUSE

Other good grouse haunts are young second growth and briar patches sprung up on burned over ground, especially those in the midst of thicker timber.

Often, among the alders, along gullies and hillsides above watered valleys, there are berries and buds that attract grouse, and here at times there is exciting hunting.

Beechnuts are a favorite dish with grouse, particularly early in the season, when smaller and tenderer. Look for the best beechnuts on the high ridges, and look for grouse there in beechnut time.

The grouse hunter, like all other upland bird hunters, who really knows the secret of success, is the one who first locates the likelist feeding spots but who also hunts all other likely looking spots encountered.

My grandfather, one of the best grouse hunters I ever knew, never passed up clumps of apple trees, or choke-cherry trees, or crab trees, in pastures, and he always sent old Sandy, a bird dog that was a bird-dog, along the grown-over stone walls, where brier and thorn apple and elder-bush and sumac produced many a dining "partridge." He knew every abandoned farm for miles around, and you will do well to "spot" them all, as they are rich in old grown up walls, old orchards, brier grown open cellars, grapes, roses, and cherries gone wild, etc., and here many a grouse will burst out for you.

GROUSE ON GROUND

In ravines but lightly grown with timber, the ground kept sweet by sunlight, seems to furnish vine and low bush growth where grouse can browse and berry and bud. Mark down these spots in your notebook, too.

To sum up—the secrets of locating grouse successfully are two: (1) Note down the likely spots in an infallible memory, or an even more infallible notebook; (2) Don't pass up any spots that look like a good feeding ground.

JACK RABBITS SPEED along at 45 miles per hour for short distances, but soon tire.

Where Timberdoodles Tarry

Secrets of Woodcock Location

As the woodcock's chief diet is worms, any cover providing ideal worm conditions attracts woodcock.

Yet it stands to reason that although you may ordinarily find the elusive "timberdoodle" in the little valleys and swales near brooks and runs, home territory for worms, there are times when conditions change, and if woodcock are absent from their usual haunts the secret of finding them is to look where unusual conditions may have sent them for temporarily better worm hunting. While this is particularly true about the "natives," the flight birds, in for a temporary stay, anyway, are even more erratic.

WOOD COCK

One old-timer, whose uncanny ability to locate woodcock is the wonder of a large section of Maine, has told me in many a confidential talk over good Scotch and soda, that if he can't flush these long-billed tid-bits among the alder runs and along the seepage borders of the small waters, he has often found them in the marginal grasses and stunted bushes on slopes arising from the runs.

That doesn't mean, however, that he didn't first follow the lines of least resistance and search the natural haunts first. His chief reliance usually was on natural cover, described by him as:

"Look for brush-lined brooks, particularly those little ones that don't grow big very fast but open up a gradually spreading out valley for themselves by zig-zagging and winding all around in their lower courses. If cows coming in for water from adjoining pasture have opened up a maze of well trampled muddy paths through the bushes, that's a good sign. Small gullies, cutting back into the slope, and well surrounded by bushes are usually a part of such an ideal set-up.

"A gentle slope to the south or west, with chumps of 'popple' and birch where the long afternoon sun streams in warmly, and here and there the ground is damp from seeping trickles, and little springs—such country holds the birds long after the frosts have driven worms deep in other sports.

"Look here for the little round drill holes, and white half-dollar size splotches of woodcock 'sign.'

"When the flight birds are in they seem to drop in to these protected slopes, rather than the denser cover, and rest before taking off again for points farther south.

"If, however, you can't locate them here, try the alders, and other brushy swales where they may have gone particularly in extra dry weather.

"I have often located woodcock, and scored a high percentage of kills, in low bush flat lands, rather soft and springy underfoot, that were once meadows apparently, but now abandoned, and bordered and liberally patched with young alders and other brush. Every bird that rises gives a clear unobstructed shot.

"Another favorite location, when birds seem absent from those I've mentioned, is sandy willow runs and sandy borders thick with water grass and long weedy vegetation on one side, and open on the other, with plenty of thick bushy country leading back from the moist sections."

Sunset and Eats

A Fable

A Poet lifted up awed eyes to the heavens, sighed,
pointed to the gorgeous sunset, and murmured:
"Ten thousand miles of shifting shades of pastel pink
and gray
Are spread across the clouds that hide the milky way.
Ten thousand miles of beauty, glowing with a golden
ray
That draws a veil across the skies to hide the dying
day."

Whereupon the Realist arose and quoth:
"The dying day is beautiful, but living hunger is
crude—
And much as I love the sunset glow, I also love my
food.
So let's give a cheer for beauty—and broil us a mess
of trout—
Or e'er the sun has passed away, I'm sure that I'll
pass out!"

—M. W. B.

Duck Distinction Secrets
How to Identify Those You Can't Shoot

Elbert Hubbard said "A dog's private life is a public disgrace," and even though we call the ways of identifying protected waterfowl "Duck Secrets" they're matters of common knowledge—to the experts! The average duck hunter knows too little about the distinguishing differences of the various kinds, and thereby either takes too many chances of violating the game laws, or else fails to shoot ducks he's really entitled to because he fears hitting a protected species.

Let's describe the wood duck first, as this duck is protected in the vast majority of our States. In fifteen States, however, you may shoot wood duck (one only) to avoid waste of one accidentally killed.

Wood Duck

Wood ducks frequent the same feeding grounds where black ducks and mallard are often shot, but are smaller than both varieties. Male and female have white, or whitish, feathers on the belly.

WOOD DUCK

Other conspicuous differences between the wood duck and the mallard and black are: wood ducks are crested (both sexes) and the males have vivid white lines on crest running from front to back. Throat patch is white, and when head is held down (which is very often and characteristic) the upper part of white throat patch appears like a white line at the jowl. Wings (both sexes) have white edge-stripes at rear, running nearly half the wing length. There is a white patch around the female's eye, and a white spur-like mark on the male's cheek. The male is the most brilliantly colored of all ducks.

The flight is faltering.

Therefore, if you see a small, crested white or whitish bellied duck, with white throat patch, white lines on head, white edged rear-of-wing, that flies falteringly, often whistling as it flies, you'll know it's a wood duck. This duck is a surface feeder.

The red-head, buffle-head, ruddy duck, and canvasback, have been recent objects of protection, and while Federal regulations have eased up on them we'll describe them, in case any quick changes are made when this year's laws are released.

Redheads and Canvasbacks

Redheads in flight look darker and smaller than canvasbacks, in fact *are* smaller, averaging from 17 to 23 inches compared to canvasbacks' 20 to 24 inches. Has to get up speed for taking flight by beating along the surface of the water before taking the air. Has a high forehead, going up from the base of the bill steeply. Bill is shorter than canvasbacks'. Head is shorter, too. They generally fly low over the water.

RED HEAD DUCK

The male, like the male canvasback, has reddish-brown head, and is mostly gray, but has a black neck and breast. The female has dull brown head and upper neck, with a reddish cast. Her upper breast and sides are brownish, with lower parts white.

CANVAS BACK

At a quick glance the general resemblance in coloration of the females might lead many hunters to confuse the redhead and the canvasback. So, too, might the general similarity in the male coloration of head and breast.

But certain differences are so marked that the experienced hunter identifies each easily.

Here are the instantly observable differences:

Canvasback	Redhead
1. Long bill, long neck give appearance of unusual length ahead of wings.	1. Short bill, stubby head, shorter neck give short appearance ahead of wings.
2. Long bill and long sloping forehead give "flat - head" impression.	2. Short bill, high forehead, give "highbrow" look!
3. Conspicuous whitish tint on male's body and wing bases give it truly "canvasback" appearance.	3. Neither sex has whitish "canvas-back."
4. A large duck, 20 to 24 inches long, with an overall wing spread of 34 to 36 inches.	4. A smaller duck, 17 to 23 inches long, with a "spread" of only 30 to 33 inches.

Ruddy Duck

These are really small ducks, averaging 13 to 17 inches, and wing-spreading only about 20 to 24 inches from tip, over back, to tip. The name is deceptive to the average hunter who doesn't see the male in his summer plumage (which really is ruddy) but in his fall and winter dress of dark gray-brown, with darker crowns. His light cheeks contrast sharply with the dark crown of his head. Both sexes have thick necks, flat heads, and spade bills. The male has stiff narrow tail feathers, which it "spreads" erect like a miniature gobbler, often when sitting on the water.

RUDDY DUCK

When rising, sputters and churns along the water, till it takes off, then flies low, with quick wing-beat, which is deceptive, as this duck, is by no means fast in comparison with really speedy quackers.

Look for it in fresh water ponds.

DUCKS that flutter, paddle, and beat along the surface of the water to get up speed for the take off into flight are mostly diving ducks, and include red-heads, bluebills, canvasbacks, ruddies, scaup, etc.

Black ducks, mallards, teal, and pintails, however, can shoot right up from the water without preliminary taxi-ing.

THE AMERICAN DUCK HAWK has been, and can be, trained for hunting, like the Old World falcon. This is the fastest flier of all American birds. Swooping, or dropping after prey, it can do over 200 miles per hour.

WHITE PELICANS hunt fish in apparently organized drives, where they herd their prey into shallow water, where the gobbling them up is easier and surer.

The Bufflehead

A little duck, so fat it is called "butterball" by many, but isn't so good eating as it suggests by its appearance. Well-named "bufflehead," as its head is very round, indeed, with a short, sharp bill for a duck. Makes a great commotion for a small bird when gaining speed for the take-off, fluttering and splashing along the surface. Has fast wing-beat, and while flying gives forth deep, guttural quacks. At first glance males look like a little black and white duck with a big head. White eye patch and splashes of white on wings are relatively large and conspicuous.

BUFFLEHEAD DUCK

The female is a toned down edition of the male in dusky brown and minus his vivid white patches and splashes.

Buffleheads are divers.

Mallards

In the opinion of plenty of wild fowlers the plump and plentiful mallard heads the list of ducks for all around cunning, size, and beauty, and comes close to his cousin, the black duck, for table qualities.

Suspicious by nature, this wariest of ducks almost never plumps straight into or alongside a bunch of decoys. Instead, they usually make several preliminary circles of inspection, then if nothing alarming appears, down they come with light splashes.

MALLARD DUCK

Two general characteristics help identify mallards in the air: the wing spread is broader than that of most ducks, and the head is smaller and more finely shaped. Most hunters recognize mallards first by their general greyish and grey brownish effect, and the characteristic purple bar which appears as if inset in the wing coverts about half way to the tips, on both males and females.

In the spring the male mallard is the easiest of all ducks to identify, as his brilliant, irridescent green head is unmistakable, and the rich brown of breast and shoulders is conspicuous. The beautiful sheen of "mallard green" has never been successfully imitated by artist, textile weaver, or jeweler. However, this fades and becomes duller in the summer and fall, but enough remains in most cases so that a keen eye can identify it. Male mallard seem to increasingly predominate in the flocks of late years. But the females are almost as easy to identify, with their prevailing grey to grey-brown mottled feathers, and the same purple wing bars as the males.

Mallards are dippers, accustomed to feed in shallow waters, and congregate closer to shore than the diving ducks. Look for them in small flag grown ponds and the shallows in larger waters where rushes and wild rice grow, also along small streams and the shallows of larger ones. Mallards, like most "dippers" take off easily, without any preliminary run along the surface. In fact they can bound straight into the air, except into an extremely stiff breeze.

Black Ducks

BLACK DUCK

On the whole, the "dusky mallard," "black mallard," or "black," as this shy "dipper" is variously called, is one of the hardest of all ducks to circumvent and bring to bag. But wary as they are, they seem at times to have strange lapses from even ordinary caution! However, if you hunt them much you can generally count on them being extremely suspicious.

While the "black" has the general configuration, broad wings, and finely shaped small head of the mallard, this fine table duck is much darker in plumage, and is easily distinguished from its cousin by its sharper quack. He is a better bird to eat than the mallard, in fact shares with the ruddy duck a distinctive flavor of his own that makes him more toothsome than almost any duck you can name.

The "black," (Anas Obscura) frequents the shallow lakes and streams in the close neighborhood of marshes, tall grass, waving rushes, and wooded shores. This writer has frequently put them up from mere spring-holes in the swamps and low brush land. They can take off in "no time at all," and get up straight into the air, unlike the diving type of ducks.

The "black" will sometimes fly straight into decoys without a preliminary circle of inspection, and in this he is totally unlike the wholly and always suspicious mallard. But don't count on any such lapse!

There are two common varieties of black ducks, the "red legs" and the common. The "red legs" seem to have not only brighter red legs but brighter yellow bills. The common black duck has duller legs with only a dull reddish touch or two on the legs, and the bills verge more to a greenish tone. Both species, male and female, have the purplish bar on the wings common to the mallard, but often this seems to border more on a bluish tinge than in the case of the mallard.

MALLARD DECOYS attract almost every other type of duck which frequents the same waters where mallards are found.

MOST BIRDS ARE "ONE-EYED," at least to this extent—they see from one eye on each side of the head, instead of focusing both eyes on things. Owls and marsh hawks are the only birds which see straight ahead with both optics.

SPRUCE "PARTRIDGE" STEAL EGGS—well, at least, the hen sometimes steals other spruce (fool) hens eggs, and sits on them as her own.

WOOD DUCKS "STUNT." Wood ducks can fly at almost full speed into the holes in trees that form their nests!

GROUSE CHICKS AND SNAKES ALIKE. The grouse chick and some varieties of baby snake, are each equipped with a spur on the end of the bill and nose, respectively (an "egg tooth") to chip and break out of the eggs from which they're born!

DUCK WINGS beat from seven to ten times per second, the smaller, low flying ducks having the fastest vibration, and flying the slowest! Their fast wing-beats, however, give the illusion of great speed.

CANVASBACKS FASTEST DUCKS. Duck speeds are greatly over-estimated. The fastest is the canvasback. In still air canvasbacks can fly 72 miles an hour when pursued at top speed. They usually fly about 50 miles per hour. With a strong following wind they can probably do about 100 miles an hour.

Secrets of Downing That Deer!

Without going into an elaborate treatise on deer hunting we want to present here a few practical, common-sense, "secrets of success" for the average fair shot on a hunting trip for deer. By deer we mean white tails, because far more of that variety are hunted in the United States and Canada than any other.

First and foremost is a pre-hunting preparatory step neglected by the majority of hunters: "sight in," or target your rifle on the range as long before you are to take your trip as possible. And then practice as many shots as you possibly can from the offhand or standing position, with your sighted-in rifle.

Target your rifle to shoot about two inches above where you aim at one hundred yards. As most of your chances in typical white tail country will be at short range, you can aim practically point blank at any deer from thirty-five to about two hundred yards and not have to allow for bullet drop. Nine-tenths of your shots will come within eighty-five yards, very few will be a hundred yards away, and almost none beyond a hundred and fifty yards.

WHITE - TAIL BUCK "GETS GOING"

Also remember that, as the .30'06 with the 180 grain bullet drops only 4.5 inches, and the .270 with the 130 grain projectile drops only 3.5 inches, at 200 yards, you'll be only a couple of inches low at 200 yards, if your rifle is sighted in to hit 2 inches above point of aim at 100 yards.

As ninety per cent of white tails are met in the woods while still hunting or driving, most of them will be moving when you see them, so your shots will have to be quickly made and entirely offhand.

The more you practice throwing off the safety (or cocking the hammer), throwing the rifle to your shoulder, and having the front sight come right on the mark, without even looking at the weapon, the better your chances on deer later. The whole process should be instantaneous, and repeated again and again, each time on a different target, until it becomes instinctive. This "dry shooting" can be practiced in your bedroom, or in any room, by imagined snap shots through the window at objects outside, after you've double-checked to be sure the rifle is absolutely not loaded! Be sure, on each practice "dry" shot also to practice getting the feel of the trigger pull, giving it a final squeeze as your front sight centers on the target. Then immediately lever or pump the mechanism, re-aim, and squeeze in a second shot.

To repeat, and emphasize, here is the routine:

1. Select the object to be aimed at quickly.
2. Throw off the safety or cock the hammer silently and bring the rifle to the shoulder, all in one decisive motion.
3. Squeeze in enough pressure on the trigger almost to set it off but not quite. You'll quickly acquire this "feel" by practice.
4. When the front sight centers on the target complete the trigger squeeze.
5. At the instant the "shot" has been "fired," lever or pump the action, aim instantly, and squeeze the trigger again.

A few minutes practice every day will make you so familiar with your rifle that its handling eventually becomes automatic, sub-conscious.

Before your rifle is sighted in, be sure you have practical hunting sights, which are an open rear sight, and a 1/8 inch ivory bead at the front. For most conditions encountered in hunting white tails, and for snap shots at moving game, where you must "draw a bead" on the target instantaneously, these sights are most practical. The Peep sight is okay—many use it—but the average shot can do quicker snap shooting, and better, with open sights.

ON RUNNING DEER

Swing the rifle with the game, and keep it swinging when you give the final squeeze to the trigger. Swing from the animal's rear, gaining with the muzzle towards the shoulders, and when the front sight reaches the front and lower chest, squeeze the trigger.

Don't stop your swing when you squeeze.

MR. WHITETAIL TAKES OFF

With modern high velocity ammunition all the "lead" you need is the gain your rifle muzzle makes as it swings from rear to front of the running animal.

GO SLOW!

Above all in hunting deer proceed slowly through the woods, or along the ridges, or open trails. At slow speed you can "freeze in your tracks" quicker, you make less noise, and your heart, nerves, and muscles will be steadier for a quick shot. When you go slowly your eyes cover more territory, and much more thoroughly, and you'll see deer you'd be sure to miss when going faster. Then again, you can keep a lot more silent when you go forward slowly and cautiously.

Avoid all sudden movements. Many times a deer which would not be alarmed otherwise is off in a panic at a sudden movement of your arms, head, or body.

One old-timer, who always gets his deer, tells me that his recipe for so doing is simply this: "I go out there, find a place where I'm not too conspicuous, and simply 'set!' Sooner or later a deer shows up, if I manage to keep silent and don't move much!"

SAFETY FIRST

Keep that safety on, or the hammer down, until you actually see game and bring your rifle up to shoot at it.

As soon as your shots are fired, or the game is out of range or sight, put that safety back on, or lower that hammer. Double-check on this last, as it is easy to forget unless you maintain constant vigilance.

UNSTEADINESS

If for any reason you are unsteady—probably due to a climb over rocks, or deadfalls, or from coming uphill—and you see a deer, you can often steady your aim by resting the left hand against a tree.

LIVE WEIGHT—DRESSED WEIGHT

The formula that if you know the live weight of a deer and take off 20% you will get the dressed weight, and conversely, if you have the dressed weight and will add 25% you will arrive at the live weight, as expressed by Dr. William A. Hornaday, has been proved erroneous by William Monpeny Newsom, whose records show that a deer loses from 26.6% to 32.5% when dressed, and that you must add from 36.4% to 48.1% of the dressed weight to get the live weight.

HOW MANY POINTS?

The average or normal number of points on a buck's antlers should be eight. The average buck reaches the heydey of strength and power anywhere from its seventh to tenth year.

WHAT ARE YOUR CHANCES OF GETTING A DEER?

According to statistics of the California Fish and Game Commission, one hunter gets his buck while two and six-tenths hunters fail!

DON'T SHOOT!

Don't shoot on suspicion that the noise you heard, or the movement you saw, might be caused by a deer. Look long. Look sharp. And unless you can be absolutely sure, don't shoot.

Also, don't shoot when the deer is too far away. Better pass him up than wound him and let him get away to suffer for days.

PRACTICE STANDING

As 50% of all white tail deer are shot from a standing position, since the brush prevents sitting or prone shots, the ambitious deer hunter should practice his shooting from the off-hand position.

Also, since about four out of ten deer are in motion (uneven, bounding, fast motion, too!), anything that will improve your running-shot percentage means more deer! Therefore, practice at moving targets, such as cans thrown into the air, cans floating down streams, moving targets in shooting galleries, and "dry shooting" (after check and re-check on having the rifle unloaded), at moving vehicles, clouds, birds, dogs, etc.

How to Rout Out Those Reluctant Rabbits!

1. The varying hare, or snowshoe rabbit, lives wherever forests grow in Canada and Alaska, and is common to many places in New England and the northern Rockies.
1. Shows white coat in winter. 2. Shows brownish summer coat.
3. The cottontail, or "cony," is found in every state in this country, in practically all the Canadian Provinces, in Mexico, and in Central America.
4. The black-tailed jack-rabbit ranges most of the less mountainous areas of the Western States. It also is found in Mexico.
5. The white-tailed jack-rabbit, or prairie hare, is found more often on the north central plains, and the lower plateaus of the American Rockies.

There's nothing complicated about hunting the most plentiful of all American game, rabbits. On the whole, the principle is: "rout out a rabbit and he'll be sure to circle back at, or near, the place he started from!"

Therefore, in hunting any kind of rabbits, whether cottontails (coneys) or the more interesting snowshoe rabbit (varying hare), the best idea is to station yourself at or near the spot you anticipate Mr. Rabbit will use as his return journey.

The strongest adjuration I can give rabbit hunters is, therefore: "Wait, wait patiently, at or near the very spot Mr. Rabbit sets out from, when he's travelling top speed to some unknown destination." And don't rush from spot to spot to spot, and try to head your quarry off! In the first place, this is nonsensical and confusing, to everybody, dogs, fellow hunters, and all others. Don't get discouraged if your beagle is silent while picking up the trail—when he finds it he'll start the music again! If he's missed it—and "Brer Rabbit" has eluded him, he'll circle till he picks up the scent again.

If you shoot and miss, you can be fairly confident that the rabbit will run approximately the same circle once more, often in the same tracks, to confuse the dog if possible.

At first this may stymie even a good dog—but a little encouragement and help from you will soon put him on the trail again.

If the rabbit is old, or an outlaw used to being hunted, he may describe a wide or erratic circle. In spite of this, your chances for a shot are better if you stay put—unless the dogs lose the rabbit's tracks altogether.

The cottontail prefers cover where he can browse on small green stuff, and being smaller, doesn't need, or choose, as thick cover as the Jack. Where one cottontail is, there are apt to be others not far away. If you start a coney and he runs into a hole somewhere, forget him and look for another—which will probably be nearby.

Should you know where his hole is, and you can get between him and his den your chances of bagging him are good.

Where both coneys and hares abound, the dog soon learns to trail whichever he starts on. But a beagle raised in Jack-rabbit territory may not take to cottontail hunting very fast—and vice versa!

The Coney remains brown, while the Varying Hare changes to white, matching the snow perfectly in Winter. The Jack-rabbit never holes up, but takes a wide circle when pursued, coming back near where he was jumped, unless deflected by hunters in your, or some other, hunting party.

If you can take along a trained rabbit dog, you'll have a lot more fun. Give me a beagle, every time in preference to a larger hound. Rabbit hunting is in his blood, and he's not so apt to get sidetracked if he crosses a fox's trail. He stays up on light crust, where the bigger hound will wallow deep in the snow. It's true that the bigger hound can negotiate heavy deep snows better and quicker—but the beagle compensates in his easiness to train, transport, and control.

When the season opens, the Jacks are apt to be widely scattered, and hard to locate, but the cold and snow drive them together in the more sheltered spruce swamps, old slashings, and spruce ridges, where they can find food and cover.

Don't go rabbit hunting in a fog or heavy rain. Your chances are mighty poor then.

When you shoot, watch out for two main points:

First: is the dog in range of your charge of shot?

Second: Swing your gun with the rabbit—creeping up on his head and shoulders from the rear. Keep the gun swinging with him even when you pull the trigger.

Important!

Handle all rabbits literally with gloves—as they may be Tularemia carriers. Cooked rabbits cannot infect you—but if you have an open sore, or eat partly cooked rabbits, you can easily pick up the disease. Disinfect, or boil your knife and any pans used to hold rabbit meat. Also disinfect the lining of your game bag, or the game pocket in your hunting coat, several times during the rabbit season.

Handle pieces of raw meat with a fork, not your fingers, and avoid getting water in which rabbit meat was soaked on your skin. Dispose of bloody water immediately and boil up your knife, and the pan.

Heat destroys the tularemia germ, but must be applied long enough to eliminate red meat and pinkish juices in centers of thick pieces.

Be careful not to crush ticks or horseflies with your fingers as they can carry tularemia germs. As horse and deer flies can carry tularemia, protect the back of your neck, and other vulnerable spots, with fly lotion, bandanna handkerchiefs, etc.

Never touch—or use—a sick, anemic, or listless rabbit.

Rabbit Lore

The Jack-rabbit—second among the really speedy American animals—has a maximum speed of about 45 miles per hour—while his worst enemy, the coyote, can do 40 miles. However, the coyote can keep up his 40 miles per hour for much longer periods than the Jack can run his 45 miles!

When a cottontail's really frightened—and puts on the pressure to go places—it quickly increases its stride from ten inches normal to 160 inches high speed!

And listen to this! The Texas Jack-rabbit has been seen to jump clean over a seven foot fence!

Byways and Dryways of Blaze-Building!

When It's Raining

Be forehanded by always carrying a little waterproof bottle or tin full of dry matches. Make it a rule never to tap this for smoking or ordinary use. Carry another larger matchbox for your ordinary uses. If this also is waterproof, so much the better.

TWO SHELLS OF DIFFERENT GUAGES MAKE A FAIRLY GOOD WATERPROOF MATCHBOX.

A good waterproof matchbox is made by fitting a ten gauge shell into a twelve gauge. But the metal or plastic boxes made specially to keep matches dry even when immersed in water are best. A cigarette lighter in the woods saves lots of matches. So do a few candles, and a flashlight.

Besides a waterproof matchbox, always with you, carry a small tightly sealed bottle packed closely with absorbent cotton (you'll be amazed how much you can cram in) into which you have finally dropped all the gasoline, benzine, or inflammable energine or other lighter-fluid the cotton will absorb.

STANDARD WATERPROOF MATCHBOX

If you only have to use this once in ten years it is well worth the trouble carrying always, as you'll be so thankful you have it in an emergency you'll thank your foresight plenty! A pinch or two drawn out of the bottle and placed under wood splinters, birch bark, resinous shavings, or a few prayer sticks will, when ignited by a match, start a fire for you in no time, even under terribly wet conditions.

Another good "igniter-helper" is a long, paraffin soaked string, cut into two inch lengths and stuffed into a bottle. You can take out as much of this as you want, and you'll find several two inch lengths, to light under the small-stuff used as a "starter," are worth their weight in gold when you need 'em!

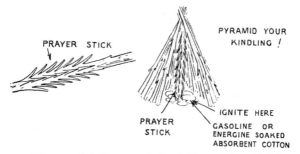

PRAYER STICK

PYRAMID YOUR KINDLING !

IGNITE HERE

PRAYER STICK

GASOLINE OR ENERGINE SOAKED ABSORBENT COTTON

"Prayer sticks" are made by taking a piece of dry wood, if you can find one in a protected spot, and raising long shavings or slivers all the way round the stick by shaving down with a sharp knife, leaving them still attached to the stick and all pointing one way in a ring of splinters which entirely surrounds one end of the stick. If you can't find a dry stick, very often you can start your fire with a seasoned stick, wet outside, but which will be dry on the underside of all the little splinters you raise.

The *modus operandi* of building the fire is to place a bit of the gasoline saturated cotton on the ground. If you use pieces of the paraffined string raise the ends up from the ground on two little parallel twigs—so you can get the match flame under the ends.

Build a little pyramid of splinters, shavings, or birch bark, above this, then put on two or three "prayer-sticks" if possible, and finally the driest pieces of split wood you can get, keeping the whole in pyramidal form as closely as possible, with all sticks, twigs and bark laid slanting and parallel up toward the peak.

Then light the cotton or paraffined string. Your care in building the pile will now be repaid, because the fire will come to life rapidly.

Don't put unsplit wood on till you have a big, strong blaze, and then eternal vigilance is the price of keeping the blaze going!

More Fire Secrets

1. Split your main match supply into several portions, and place each in a different pack, canoe, or duffel bag. Then in case of mishap, only part of the supply is lost.

2. As a precaution matches can be dipped into paraffin, then placed in several waterproof containers.

THREE OR FOUR
MATCHES STRUCK
WHEN HELD TIGHT-
LY TOGETHER -
MAKE A FIERCER
FLAME.

CAREFUL :
DON'T BURN
YOUR FINGERS

3. Often two or three matches held closely together and struck all at once will stay lit in a strong wind or rain where a single match will be extinguished.

4. In case your entire supply of matches is lost you can obtain fire from firearms ammunition as follows: pry out the bullet from a rim-fire cartridge with your fingers. You may have to cut off the bullet, at the end of the jacket, with center fire cartridges, and pry out the base with your knife. If you can't work this, split the shell neck carefully with your belt axe. Shotgun shells can be cut off level with the top powder wad, and the wads pried out with knife-point.

Then pour out most of the powder, in a dry place, sprinkling some of it (only a few grains in one place) among the shavings or tinder you have assembled to start your fire.

Leave only a little less powder in the shell than is normally used to load a twenty-two long rifle cartridge. Wad a dry cotton rag (not wool) into the shell, on the powder left there, and tamp firmly in place.

Load the gun, point skyward, fire. The smoldering wad of cloth which falls to the ground should be blown on gently till it flames and placed lightly as close to and under your "starter" kindling as possible. Don't stuff it in roughly and forcibly, as you are apt to extinguish the flame you have started with so much trouble.

WHAT WOOD FOR FIRES
And Where to Find It

Even in rainstorms certain inner barks keep dry and inflammable. Dead, seasoned timber will keep dry inside, even when very wet on the surface. Look for such wood in windfalls that don't touch the ground and absorb dampness, in lightning or fire killed trees, or in large dead limbs on live trees. Split or shave off the soaked outside of such woods and you'll have dry, inflammable wood beneath.

Small, dead limbs on the lower trunks, especially of evergreens, are often sound and seasoned. Break them off and into short pieces. The breaks will be ragged and dry and catch fire easily. A little additional shaving off of wet exteriors helps, or you can shave splinters to stand up in one direction, making "prayer sticks."

Look for dry birch bark especially in sheltered spots. Examine overhanging banks, rocks, leaning logs, small caves, cliffs, hollow trunks.

Use Hard Woods

Hard woods burn into live coals instead of ashes, like soft woods, and furnish steadier, longer, more intense heat. Seasoned hickory and white ash are swell firewoods. Maple and live, red, and white oak run a close second. Hemlock bark is a good campfire fuel— it burns down to good red cooking coals. Black birch, locust, beech, cherry are alternatives, not bad, in case of "have-to."

Soft woods are good fire starters, poor finishers.

Some green woods will make hot fires, especially if split. These are hickory, ash, and maple. Soft pine, cedars, sassafrass, tamarack, and spruce, snap and spark too much for safety or comfort. Avoid elm for fuel.

Don't build fires against fallen trees or logs, for safety's sake. Clear away all dry leaves, grass, etc., around your fire for about four feet. Build fires on bare ground, containing no humus, roots, leaves or grass, to smolder after you leave, or spread smouldering fire into surrounding combustibles.

Take double precautions to extinguish all traces of spark, smoulder, and flame when you leave.

In strong winds build only a small fire, and watch closely. A round hole, a foot and a half deep is the safest fireplace in such circumstances.

In somewhat lesser winds dig two intersecting trenches about 3½ feet long, seven or eight inches wide and a foot deep. Build your fire at the intersection, and lay flat stones on each corner here to place kettle or skillet on.

CANADA GEESE can fly 60 miles an hour when frightened. They normally cruise about 50 miles per hour. A Canada goose will weigh from seven to twelve pounds, with not many twelve pounders.

Secrets of Canoe-Safety

If a canoe capsizes, stick with it! Why desert your nearest available help to keeping afloat just because you've had an unexpected accident?

Wooden craft don't sink. There's enough buoyancy in even a capsized canoe to keep you afloat for weeks, if necessary!

If you will make it an inflexible rule "no more than three" to a canoe, you may one day be mighty glad. Although even a sixteen-footer will support four people when overturned in the water, if one is at each end, one on each side, and everybody relaxes as much as possible to allow his own body buoyancy full play, three persons to a canoe can feel a lot safer. In the first place, the chances of a capsize are less with three aboard than with four. And if an overturn comes three are better off for buoyancy.

If I had my way, however, two persons to a canoe would be the absolute limit! Two in a canoe are safer than one, even, because, properly seated, two people trim the craft better, and make it more controllable in a wind.

WHEN A STRONG WIND CATCHES YOUR CANOE HERE, OVER YOU GO!

ROCK OR SANDBAG HERE BALANCES WEIGHT KEEPS BOW DOWN.

The chief fundamental for safe one-man or one-woman operation of a canoe is to weight down the bow, with several large rocks. I have pulled so many greenhorns who didn't do this out of the water that the fact sticks up in my mind like a sore finger. Each time the canoe was overturned because the single occupant got caught in a high wind, and, sitting in the stern with no ballast in the bow, which stuck way up and caught the full force of the wind, tried in vain to keep the bow from turning with the wind. Desperate paddling does no good, and when a harder gust than usual comes, over goes the canoe!

Of course anyone who understands canoes would have changed from the back to just forward of the middle and, kneeling there, could have controlled the craft, even in a very strong wind.

But the civilized man's knees are tender, and although the kneeling position for a solo paddler is the safest, I have always felt perfectly safe, and certainly more comfortable, when seated at ease in the stern, with rocks holding the bow down in the water and out of the wind.

No matter how good a canoeman you are there may come a blow when the only sensible thing you can do, if out on big water, is to lie down on the canoe bottom. There you will be perfectly safe, in the wildest lake storm, and sooner or later you absolutely must be blown ashore!

Speaking of one person paddling, here is a real secret —not known to one in a hundred average canoemen. If you want your canoe strictly controllable, with much less effort on your part, put enough ballast in the bow to bring it just a little lower in the water than the stern, with you in it. You'll discover then that you can pivot a lot easier on the bow than you could on the stern, with considerably less paddle-power!

WOODCOCK ARE UNBELIEVABLY SLOW. The slowest flier of all American game birds is the woodcock, which does anywhere from five to twenty miles per hour, depending how hard pressed he is. The woodcock's upper bill is flexible, and movable at the tip, so that it is almost finger-like in its ability to grasp worms. You can tell the woodcock's sex by the length of its beak: more than 2¾″ long means female, and if less than 2¼″ male, usually. The in-betweens can't be identified by bill length.

MARSH RABBITS SWIM in the water of their native Southern swamps with only eyes, nose, and top of head showing. They make tunnels through matted grass and undergrowth for runways.

Baffle That Ivy Itch!

Secrets of Curing Ivy Poison Revealed

Nothing can so quickly convert a joyous hunting or fishing trip into a painful and lugubrious "bust" as ivy poisoning, which, when extensive, can be acutely dangerous, as well as disagreeable.

The treatment here described is heroic, but sure fire.

Take along a small bottle of household ammonia. When you know you've touched poison ivy, sop the area affected with plenty of the undiluted ammonia. This will kill the ivy acid, which is the disturbing factor of this particular irritation.

If the characteristic tiny, whitish, itching, blisters have already appeared, break them by briskly rubbing with a clean cloth or handkerchief, and apply plenty of the full strength ammonia. The alkali will burn, but it will immediately neutralize the ivy acid. This severe treatment should be used only when the area affected by the poison is not too widespread. Any large poisoned area, where the blisters are deep, and the case aggravated, may be treated with the ammonia diluted by from 1/3 to 2/3 water. If the case is very severe, and covers an extremely large area, indeed, the patient should consult a doctor.

However, if you always have the ammonia along, you can usually "break up" the poisoning at the start. As ivy poisoning spreads rapidly when the first blisters break and carry the infection to adjoining areas, the quicker you apply your ammonia the better.

A five per cent solution of ferric chloride in 50% alcohol, dabbled over the face and hands, and allowed to dry on, is an almost sure antidote, when applied before exposure to ivy poisoning. Or a strong solution of ferrous sulphate may be employed, in the same way.

However, you will need to renew your application soon to keep it effective, if the weather is hot and you perspire much.

Both the ferric chloride and ferrous sulphate are good remedies, if used directly after exposure, and in 9 cases out of 10 will kill the poison completely.

The most foolish thing you can do is to follow the ancient and very wrong advice to eat poison ivy to immunize yourself, or neutralize the poison after contact. This may result in severe alimentary infection, or death.

If you have been exposed to ivy poisoning it is often a wise precaution, if you are extremely sensitive to the plant, to bathe the whole body in the ferric chloride solution, as this will scotch the poison where it may have been contacted without your knowledge.

Persons sensitive to poison ivy may usually keep free from its effects by keeping a vigilant watch out for it. Suspect every three leaved plant you see, particularly if glossy green, or green and reddish. "Leaflets three— let it be!" is a good rule to follow strictly. The writer, who is particularly sensitive to ivy, has avoided being poisoned by it for the last seven years by keeping a keen eye suspiciously on all three leaved vines and shrubs, and keeping away from them. In trout fishing, particularly, he looks over every few yards of the bank before entering the area.

SHUN ALL PLANTS WITH THE LEAVES GROWING IN THREES !

To "Silence" Skunk Scent

Many hunters, and other dog owners, don't know the simplest, and at the same time, most effective, of all the odor-quashers, for a dog which has, alack, encountered this noisome member of the weasel family.

THE VINEGAR WORKS

Strong vinegar is the answer. Wash the affected parts in bulk cider vinegar. If the bottled vinegar you have is too weak to neutralize the odor at the first washing, rinse thoroughly and use it again! Results are immediate, perfect, and very comforting.

No need to bury your own clothes, or throw them away, if you should be so rash, unwise, or unfortunate as to come within range of a barrage laid down by a "Hyacinth Kitty!"

Just wash 'em out in strong vinegar. If this should remove some of the color remember this: it will also eradicate ALL of the odor!

Lost? You Can be Found!

First thing to do, if you think you're lost, is to sit down and try to figure out where you are. Keep cool!. Look around for landmarks. Is there a mountain which dominates the surrounding country? Doesn't this give you a cue where you are? How about that stream near-by? Don't you know where it comes out? Isn't the sun, setting over there, as good as a compass, because that direction is, has been, and always will be, West! Conversely, you can be darned sure that, even if the sun has sunk out of sight, and you have to wait till morning, you can then know where East is, as the sun comes up there, and in no other direction!

But suppose you don't know which way to go, even if you know what the directions are? Well, if there's a stream you can follow it downstream, and it will usually come out in some town.

Hunger may bother you, but even so you needn't fear starving to death. At least not for several weeks! Don't you know that a normal, or even sub-normal person, can fast for twenty days, and many people can go without food for thirty days, or more, and not suffer serious, or permanent effects?

If you are lost, and night is coming on, find some sort of shelter, the lee of a big rock, fallen big tree, etc., then clear away all inflammables for three or four feet and build a fire, which will do a lot to keep your morale cheerful, and your body comfortable.

If it's cold, and you haven't a blanket, build your fire in a two foot wide trench about six inches deep. When you have a bed of coals cover with earth, and sleep on the warm spot.

If you've no means of starting a fire (see article on Page 113 in this booklet) cover yourself with leaves, or with plenty of pine or cedar branches.

To signal for help remember the standard Forestry and Outdoorsmen's codes. Here they are:

Sound Signals: Three quick shots from any firearm, three quick shouts, or three quick whistles. Forestry Service suggests every sportsman carry a shrill whistle, whose blast is much more penetrating than a voice, and which can be blown without much, or exhausting effort.

Sight Signals (Daytime): Three puffs of smoke, from a fire built where it won't start a forest conflagration. Throw damp wood or green leafy branches on it to make smoke, and regulate the puffs wtih your coat, or a blanket. Three mirror flashes; or waving a coat, shirt, or blanket (use something white if possible) in three wide semi-circles.

Sight Signals (Night): Three small fires in a row, three flashes from a flashlight, or from screening and unscreening a lantern, or a small, bright fire.

Be sure to keep repeating all signals at regular intervals in order to attract attention by their recurrence. The three fires, however, should be kept burning steadily.

There are three indispensables when you go into big woods, hunting, fishing, or hiking. These are compass, map, and matches in a waterproof box.

I know one very successful resort owner, who at the expense of about 50c for each guest, insists that each one, even when accompanied by a guide, carry with him the topographical map of the region prepared by the lumber company which operates there. Such maps, or the Government's Geodetic Survey maps are available for almost every part of the country, no matter how wild or unsettled. With such a map, and a compass, even a tenderfoot can find his way out, especially if he will check his course occasionally during the day by some prominent landmark. If, however, no landmark is available, he should check before going out something like this: "Here's the camp on the stream which flows north to south. I'm hunting east of it today. To get back to the stream, I can't miss if I go west. I'll just glance at the compass now and then and see how much I veer north or south. Then if I am lost temporarily at any time I'll just go west and reach the stream, and I already have checked enough to know that by veering north I'm going to come out above camp. So I'll go downstream till I get there."

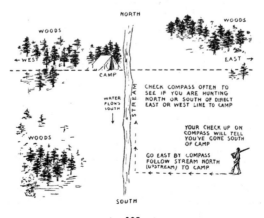

Another good stunt to avoid being lost is to mark out on the map in pencil certain parallel or converging trails, or a triangle between two streams, or a circle around a hill beyond which you positively forbid yourself to go.

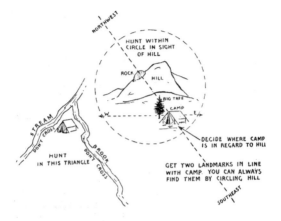

Above all, when a guide places you on a ridge, trail, runway, or stand, stay right there. Don't even go twenty yards to one or the other side of it.

Should you be darn fool enough to follow a wounded animal, or for some other reason stray from the spot, stop where you are and stay there the moment you're "lost." If you do this you'll hear the guide the minute he returns, finds you absent, and shouts for you. Certainly you won't be out of distress signal range. But don't start firing distress signals till its time for the guide to return to the spot where he placed you. Save your ammunition for the time when it will do some good.

Another thing—if you come into camp late the night of your arrival, and next day is sunless, better be sure you are all straightened out by a guide or the proprietor on north, east, south and west, as you may have some absurd ideas about direction, due to being "turned around," and no sun, etc.

Also, any man who goes into big forest without knowing how to build fires, utilize shelter, etc., is just plain foolish. Practice at these tasks till you know their fundamentals at least, before starting out.

Above all, you have reasoning power. So why fly into a senseless panic? Even if you spend a night or two in the woods, do your travelling by day, and avoid risking a broken leg, sprained ankle, or other hurt.

If you're incapacitated by an accident, anyway, the best thing you can do is to stay right where you are, build a big fire and keep it smoking as constantly and as much as you can, by throwing on green brush. Chances are this will be seen and investigated, especially now that most Forestry Services are equipped with planes, which can easily locate, and always report, where distress signals (above all smoke) are coming from!

Life-Saving Secrets

No matter how careful you, or others, may be with hunting knives, axes, and firearms in the woods, every now and then an accident happens. If that accident should happen on *your* trip, a knowledge of what to do may mean the life of a valued pal, or some stranger, who may be somebody else's valued pal.

Here are the essentials of one most important first aid—stopping the flow of blood.

If the cut or wound has severed an artery the blood comes in pumping rhythm, in time with the heart beat. If a vein has been injured, the blood comes more steadily. Arterial blood is brighter.

General rule is: pressure between the wound and the heart to stop arterial blood loss; pressure between the wound and the extremities to stop veins bleeding.

Focal point to stop bleeding at the temples, or in the scalp, is just in front of the ear and above the hinge of the jaw. This is the most puzzling of all bleeding places to the average man of no medical knowledge. In general the fingers or thumbs have to be used for first aid here, to maintain the pressure.

Tourniquets can be most easily applied to arms or legs. The main arm arteries are in the forearm, high up on the inside, and the tourniquet pressure should be brought here.

The principal leg arteries come near the surface in the thigh, high up on the inner side, just a little below the fold in the groin.

Make tourniquets from a handkerchief, or a folded strip of shirt or shorts, with a small round stone, a small chip of wood, or a knot in the cloth, placed to press on the artery. A stick passed under the tourniquet will when twisted serve to tighten the band, but must be loosened for a few moments about every quarter hour, to avoid ruptured veins or future gangrene.

Unless the wound is a tremendous one, your stopping the bleeding with a tourniquet, or hand pressure, will allow time for coagulation. Then iodine, mercurochrome, chlorozene solution, or other good disinfectant in solution may be applied. Be careful not to apply corrosive or acid disinfectants in such strength as to destroy tissues.

A sterile bandage then applied will help protect the wound from reopening. If you haven't an emergency kit, but do have iodine or other disinfectant, a single layer clipping of cloth wet with the disinfectant may be applied directly to the wound, and the main bandage torn from an outside shirt or clean handkerchief then put on.

On all woods trips it is best to prepare in advance for most eventualities and to have, at least in camp, a well chosen emergency kit.

While some of the items will be indispensable in a serious emergency, many of them can contribute far beyond their cost in mitigating some of the small annoyances and accidents.

Therefore, be foresighted about such common camp misfortunes as sunburns, fire burns, blisters, minor cuts, bites, ivy poison, sprains, chafing, cold sores, chapped lips, colds, indigestion, etc.

Check with the following list and include the items in your "emergency chest," which will all fit into a very small tackle box:

1. Either ferrous sulphate, or ferric chloride (for ivy or poison sumac (poison oak).
2. Vaseline.
3. Boric Acid.
4. Borated Powder.
5. Eye Cup.
6. Antiseptic Salve.
7. Camphor Ice.
8. Licorice Powder.
9. Fly Dope.
10. Warming liniment, or oil and wintergreen.
11. Absorbent Cotton.
12. 2 rolls surgical bandage (1″ and 2″).
13. 2″ adhesive (may be torn or cut for ½″ to 1″ tape).
14. Box of "Band-aids."
15. ½ Doz. applicators.
16. Bottle of chlorozene tablets (disinfectant) or permanganate of potash tablets.
17. Glycerine or sweet oil.
18. 2 Dozen Aspirin tablets.
19. Bicarbonate of Soda.

20. Iodine or Metaphen.
21. Tube of tannic acid jelly.
22. Toothache drops.
23. Scissors.
24. Tweezers.
25. Small mirror.
26. Safety razor blades.

Why not enclose with this a good book on First Aid and the Red Cross booklet on artificial respiration in water accidents?

Foot-Comfort Cues
for Campers

Sore, blistered, aching, or cold feet can run you right out of all enjoyment on your fishing, hunting, or camping trip.

First let's get at a few old-timers' secrets for warm weather foot comfort.

First and foremost—Wool socks, as heavy as practicable, that fit. All the real woods experts and guides wear 'em, because they absorb shock, abrasion, and perspiration.

Second but also foremost—Shoes that fit, as heavy as practicable. They avoid tired, bruised feet, and ease shocks and fatigue.

Third and equally important—Clean socks, clean feet, for comfort. They keep your feet in tip-top hygienic trim, and avoid several discomforts.

Fourth and not one jot behind—Instant attention to blisters, chafed spots, corns, and callouses. Otherwise many ills result.

Let's take 'em all up in the order above.

The "Key of Komfort" in the woods, afield, canoeing and on the water is those soft, pure all-wool, heavy socks that all experienced woodsmen wear. They cushion the feet, top and bottom, fore and aft. They absorb shoe friction. They take up stone shock and bruises. They absorb perspiration, and, even when your boots and socks are wet, they retain warmth. Take enough pairs with you so you can always change into clean dry socks. Socks should be neither too long nor too short. Too long, they wrinkle and crease. Too short, they crowd the toes, and cause aches. The width will take care of itself. So choose socks a comfortable fit, with easy but not surplus length. Choose them heavy, "hand-knit," if possible, and soft wool, not too tightly knit. Gray, white and natural undyed, are best. The average tenderfoot thinks woods socks are too heavy, but in them his feet will be so much more comfortable, even on the hottest day, and he can hike so much farther, easier, and efficiently, that he'll be converted for life after one trip's contrast with the blisters, cold feet, chafed feet, sweaty feet, and other ills induced by thin cotton socks.

When you try on hunting shoes at your dealer's be sure to take along a pair of heavy woods socks, put them on over your ordinary socks, and then size up your footgear accordingly. If everything feels comfortable, not too snug, not too loose, with your civilian socks under your woods hose, your shoes are just about right. Judge comfort by standing and taking a few steps, not when just sitting. The thin socks inside the outing pair will be just enough to make allowance for the slight swelling which all sustained tramping in the woods will bring to your feet.

Don't choose too long hunting or hiking boots. They can become terrifically uncomfortable when you are seated in a boat for long hours, as they bind the upper calf. Six to eight inch tops are high enough for all usual woods purposes, and although twelve inch tops are still comfortable, anything beyond that is a mistake, unless you have to wear higher boots in snake infested country.

6 INCH TOP MOST COMFORTABLE. THEY DON'T BIND THE LEG.

The soles should be heavy enough to protect your city-soft feet thoroughly from trail rocks, roots, etc.

Too large shoes cause blisters by friction, but too large shoes are better than too small, because you **CAN** remedy looseness by wearing a thin pair of socks under your heavy ones, but cramping shoes you never can make comfortable. An innersole inserted in too large shoes will often entirely remedy sloppy fit. Shoes should be full forward, but absolutely snug at the heel. Otherwise you have to lace them too tight across the instep for fit.

PRONG HORNS RUN sixty miles an hour when pressed. This antelope is the fastest animal in either North or South America. It can hold 40 miles per hour for long runs.

Clean feet, clean socks, make such a tremendous difference, on long hikes, or even medium hikes! The removal of the by-products of perspiration by daily washing both of feet and socks prevents a lot of foot discomfort, and much infection in cuts or sudden blisters that break. If you have to choose, where time  is limited, on a quick hike, between clean feet and clean socks daily, take the clean socks! Soft clean socks are a constant joy for comfort and morale, not to mention aesthetics!

Blisters and callouses and corns can nullify all the money you've spent for good equipment, transportation, licenses, and guides, and tired, aching feet will smash your whole trip flat as a pancake!

You would be wise, before going on a woods trip, if your corns or callouses are in bad shape, to take a week or two of treatment from a good chiropodist. This would cost little compared to your increased and sure enjoyment.

Blisters can be forestalled and prevented if you put a strip of adhesive tape or a Band-aid on the irritated spot the minute you notice it. Blisters already developed should be opened at one edge with a needle, pin, or awl, sterilized in a match flame. After the water is pressed out and wiped away, a small thin layer of absorbent cotton can be placed over the blister, on a layer

"RUBBER-BOTTOM" TYPE WILL KEEP FEET DRY IN MELTING SNOW.

of surgical gauze resting directly on it, and all this held in place by adhesive tape, or a Band-aid can be placed with the treated spot directly on the blister.

BLISTER NEEDLE STERILIZED IN MATCH FLAME

OPEN BLISTER AT THE EDGE (NOT MIDDLE) TO AVOID SKIN RUBBING OFF LATER

If a blister seems forecast between the toes by chafing and irritation, a tiny layer of cotton, or a Band-aid wound around the toe at the irritated spot, will prevent the formation of the blister.

Often when chafing or friction develops you can soap both the shoe at the spot, and the sock where it rubs on it, and ease the discomfort and forestall the blister.

Avoid soaking feet in hot water as this makes them tender. Be sure any foot powder you use is toughening instead of softening.

The average city man would do well to avoid spring heels, and soft soles in all woods boots.

If you like rubber-bottoms, but rubber doesn't like your feet, you can avoid all its discomfort by "drawing the feet" many times by a leather innersole. This also takes up many a shock and bruise.

Frequently, when there's a roughness at some spot, on a seam, or at the toe, or sole, or heel, you can pound and smooth it down with a rounded stone, placed on it, while you tap the outside of the shoe, over the spot.

Cold Weather Foot-Comfort

Felt boots, kept dry by rubber bottoms, are the warmest footgear for ice fishermen. Two medium weight pairs of pure wool socks inside any winter boots are warmer than one heavy pair, but one medium pair and one heavy pair are still warmer.

Rubber bottoms are the only ones that will exclude the pervasive wet of melting snow. Even the best of "waterproof" leather can't keep your feet dry in the slush and wet of ice fishing under most conditions when it's good.

Expensive socks really are the only truly warm ones, as they are pure wool, and not the shoddy, non-insulating type, containing wool fillers, grease, and what-not.

HEAVY WOOL SOCKS ARE A "MUST"

Before you go out, if you rub your feet with snow in a warm room, and then dry briskly with a rough towel, they'll tingle with warmth for hours!

If your foot circulation isn't vigorous, in fact is below par, try the above before going out, and wear a pair of thin wool socks next the feet, a medium pair over these, and a heavy pair last. You must be sure your boots are big enough to take all this covering easily, as tight fitting footwear causes more cold feet than too little covering!

Often changing to dry socks at noon will keep your feet warm for the rest of the day, particularly if your feet perspire freely.

Do you know the quickest and best way to get your feet warm if your footwear is waterproof? Break the ice on stream or pond and hold your feet (inside the boots, of course) in the water! The air may be zero or less—but the water is never below 32°!

Goodbye Gun-Shyness

Secrets of Avoiding and Curing It!

An almost sure "immunization treatment" to avoid gun-shyness is to begin by firing a cap-pistol for several days every time you feed the puppy. Perhaps the best way is to have someone else do the firing, as this avoids all disagreeable impressions that the sudden noise at a pleasant mealtime is made by the hand that brings the food. However, that is "stretching it pretty fine," and nine out of ten puppies can be taught to associate the delights of food with the inevitable crack of the cap. After a few days of this, a twenty-two rifle can be substituted for the cap-pistol.

Here is the procedure. Show the food to the puppy first and let him smell it, so his whole attention is wrapped up in the approaching meal. While he wags his tail at the prospect of good "eats," have your helper fire the cap pistol at first, and then, in a day or two, the .22.

Soon you can fire the shot yourself to announce your coming with the food, and the puppy will get in the habit of associating the gun with feeding time, and will look forward to the sharp signal that mealtime has once more put in an appearance.

After the pup is accustomed to the small report of the

.22 rifle, you can change to a heavier calibre, or a blank-cartirdge shot gun report.

If you once start this method keep it up as a signal it is time to eat. Don't skip it for a day, or even a meal, if you want the lesson to sink in.

If you want to skip this precautionary treatment, or you didn't acquire your young dog till he was over six months old, you can start his education and familiarity with firearms in the field.

Most important step is to make sure the young dog has faith and confidence in you by uniformly kind and patient treatment, petting, and feeding him yourself. Then take him afield and let him find and get acquainted with game, not once, but many times, before you even think of shooting the light rifle, or lightly loaded blank in a shotgun.

First let him find game. Then, when he flushes it and chases it, fire the gun in the air while he is concentrated on the escaping birds. The pup which has never even heard a gun before will not be afraid under these conditions—at least 99 out of a hundred won't be! And he will never develop gun-shyness if his education is managed intelligently from then on.

If you can kill one or two birds over him, his pleasant association of the report with game achieved is all the more help. But even in closed season, when you can't kill game, the puppy's concentration on and interest in the pursuit of game, will take his mind entirely off the sudden noise of the firearm, and, if you repeat the firing for a while, every time he's absorbed in game and the chase, he'll before long consider the noise as an actual part of the pursuit of game.

Guard against taking out a nervous, timid young dog and shooting over him prematurely. Be sure he's actually seen and actually chasing game. You can do your training on holding point and all that later. The main essential is to be sure he's gun-acquainted, gun-tolerating, gun-and-game associating, for what good is all other training if he's gun-shy?

Never give a young dog his first introduction to gun-report after having chastised him, or soon after any disagreeable experience. Better wait an hour or so till he's able to get fully interested in game, and fully trusts you and is confident of your all important friendship and protection.

Avoid going afield with a newly purchased dog, tired and nervous from a journey, or as yet unacquainted with you and his new environment. If he was never gun-shy before, this is the time to make him decidedly that way! Far better wait till you win his affection and confidence.

In case of doubt—if you're not sure he has been game-and-gun broken-in—don't, above all else, fire a shot to see if he's gun shy. That's a swell way to make him fear a gun. Be safe, sure, and cautious, therefore, and proceed with his game finding before you fire a shot over him.

To Cure Gun-Shyness

An ounce of prevention is worth a ton or so of attempted cure in the case of gun-shyness, which is a pretty difficult fault to eradicate once it develops.

It is perhaps easier, if curing gun-shyness can be called easy under any circumstances, to cure a bird dog or beagle than a fox-hound.

Let's take the tougher proposition first. The big problem in the case of a gun-shy fox-hound is killing a fox he is chasing, close enough to him so he can see that the gun shot is really his friend and ally in the killing of the game. That is a pretty tough thing to arrange, but is about the only procedure which stands much chance of success. As you don't want a fox-hound to chase anything but a fox, this makes your problem all the harder.

In the case of pointers, or setters, the best procedure seems to be to leave your gun home for several trips, and do all you can to gain the dog's interest in hunting, finding game, and coming staunchly to point. If you can have the gun-shy dog hunt with another good dog eager for hunting, this often quickens and increases your own dog's desire for hunting and pleasure from finding game. Plenty of praise and petting when your dog finds game, and holds it to point, increases his friendship and confidence.

If and when your dog has become an enthusiastic hunter, the crucial time comes when you should go in and shoot a bird he has pointed. You can't afford to miss. If you are not a pretty accurate wing shot perhaps you can get a friend who is to take care of this shot—which should above all not be missed. But make sure that you have previously accustomed the dog to your friend, and that he has handled and praised the dog, and won his friendship, on several previous hunts without a gun.

Spaniels can many times be cured of gun-shyness by hunting them with another good hunting dog about their size, doing all the hunting without guns until your dog has shown he is really eager and interested. If the other dog is a first class hunter, his enthusiasm often inspires the gun-shy dog. When your dog has become really enthusiastic and eager, you should fire a pistol cap, or very light blank, every time the two dogs rouse up rabbit or bird. From pistol cap or lightly loaded blank you can progress gradually to heavier loaded blanks, till at last you can fire a fully loaded shell and kill game.

Meantime you should do everything possible to increase the bond of friendly understanding and confidence between you and the dog.

Wing-Shooting Formulae

Secrets of Success—and Safety

The secret of being able to shoot longer into the twilight, both when the shadows lengthen into night and when age begins to creep up on a man, is to learn to be a "pointer," not an aimer, with your shotgun. This also is one secret of making the average gunner an effective, practical, wing-shot.

Learn, if you possibly can, not to try to sight along the barrel and line up with the bird, or to ride it out. Shoot with both eyes wide open, with instinct guiding the gun.

You'll make a lot of misses, especially at the beginning. Keep on instinctively looking wide-eyed at the flying bird and instinctively bringing the gun to bear on it.

You'll never be a record-breaking shooter this way, but probably you'll get to a point where you can hit the quick ones, the instantaneous get-aways, the unexpected burster-uppers, with a lot more success than if you tried to coach yourself along to aim carefully at 'em!

The co-ordination of this instinctive snap shooting is generally a matter of keeping at it. Sooner or later your gun points nearer the bird your eyes follow, not only nearer, but oftener nearer! And the scattering shot do the rest.

A wing shot who learns gun pointing rather than aiming is never bothered half so much by dense shadows, or obstructed light, in thick growth. Nor do dull dark days, or early light, or late dusk handicap him so much. And when years creep upon him and his sight isn't so keen, he can still point and hit, through his years of pointing co-ordination and practice, just so long as he can see or sense the direction of the moving bird.

Sooner or late, by keeping at it, the gun has become a part of you, and instinct does about everything.

Speaking of instinct, learn the hard, sure way, always to keep the safety on. This you can do even when walking up on a bird held to point by your dog. If you keep the safety on, you'll learn by repetition to slap it off all in the same instant the bird flushes and you point your gun at him. It takes time to describe it, but it's all done instinctively, quicker than you can think about it, if you have persistently practiced it. For a long time you'll miss 'em—take "dry shots" at 'em, but all of a sudden, after faithful practice, it will all come to you, and you'll flash off safety, clip gun to shoulder, point, and shoot, all in a fine split second.

This is the secret of continual safety as well as the ability to bring down unexpected flushes. No unexpected stumble, no bee sting, no jump of dog, no falling branch, nothing will cause a premature gun shot. And when you do everything together in a split second you'll nail many an unexpected bird that flushes out of nowhere. On the other hand, if you're accustomed to taking off the safety lesisurely, when you start to walk in on a bird held at point, you'll be all at sea when a sudden one explodes from nowhere, and you'll fumble the safety surprisingly.

MOOSE TROT even when hard pressed. They could go faster, if like the elk, they would gallop when pursued. The elk, as a general rule, proceeds when in a hurry by trotting.

Secrets of Conquering Dog Distemper

Good news for owners of valuable dogs (what dog you've owned very long isn't valuable?—at least in *your* estimation!) is the information that sulfapyridine and sulfathiazole are apparently the answers to the veterinaries' prayer for a sure distemper cure.

Eighty-three recoveries out of eighty-seven cases from canine distemper, the greatest and deadliest dog disease, followed the controlled treatment with sulfapyridine and sulfathiazole of dogs which were in the early stages of the disease. Treated when the symptoms of this malignant disease were recognized, most of the canines treated recovered inside five days, and the temperature was normal two days after the initial treatment.

In all fairness, however, it should be stated that puppies under two months old, and dogs with chronic distemper, failed to respond to the magic of the "sulfa" drugs.

If your dog, therefore, shows any signs of distemper, you can with the aid of a qualified veterinary, be almost sure of a cure, provided treatment is undertaken at once.

The four forms of distemper are: pectoral (head, nose, eyes, and lungs affected); nervous (continued convulsions); intestinal (profuse diarrhea, even to the passage of blood), and the skin form.

Distemper symptoms are rigors, sneezing, dullness, loss of appetite, desire for warmth, and increased temperature, respiration, and pulse. The eyes are red, and the nose at first dry and harsh, becomes smeared with the discharge which soon begins to flow from the nostrils. Suppuration also is noticed in the eyes, and vision is more or less impaired by the mucus and pus, and often the very cornea itself becomes ulcerated, with eventual perforation in some cases. A cough sets in, which in some cases is violent enough to induce vomiting.

Whenever any or several of these symptoms are noticed the veterinary should be called in and the controlled dosage and use of sulfapyridine and sulfathiazole begun. The development of the "sulfa" treatment, however, is so recent that it is doubtful if all veterinaries know the entire regimen. It might, therefore, be wise to seek out one who does.

The concensus among veterinaries seems to be that immunization is really the best way to guard your dog against distemper, and that the best treatment is the Laidlaw-Duncan serum, which can be secured only by licensed graduate veterinarians.

Intriguing Info About Hunting and the Hunted

BELLING FOXES is done by having one of a party trailing Reynard over the snow carry a six inch bell, which he rings constantly, and easily. Under such circumstances the wily fox saves his strength by keeping not far ahead of his slow trailers. A man on horseback, or a fast walker then circles far ahead of the hunt and ambushes the fox.

DEER RUMINATE. Are you, like most sportsmen who have never closely observed deer, surprised to learn that they really "chew their cuds?"

THEY'RE WEASELS. Do you know that the skunk, the wolverine, and the tiny weasel, all belong to the same family?

THERE ARE ONLY ABOUT 5,000 BUFFALO of all the countless millions that once inhabited our western plains. The Eastern bison, black and humpless, is entirely extinct.

PYGMY RABBITS, which are only a foot long, inhabit Idaho and adjoining States.

DEER CAN CRY, as they have lachrymal glands like human beings.

BIG BULL ELK herd the females and all smaller elk into the valleys when deep snows arrive. They locate and drive down any strays from the main herd.

MANY OWLS ARE PRIMARILY
RODENT HUNTERS

Owls are over-rated, over condemned, as game bird predators. Most of them are also not so damaging to poultry as most people believe. Their chief articles of diet are usually mice, rats, frogs, insects, etc.

HORNED OWL

SHORT EARED OWL

BARN OWL

DRAWINGS FROM
NATIONAL SPORTSMAN

Perhaps only one, the Great Horned Owl, is really destructive to game birds and small animals in most of the United States. This owl is big enough and fierce enough to be really dangerous to the roosting poultry, game birds, and small game like rabbits, hares, and squirrels.

The owl oftenest seen by sportsmen, the Short Eared Owl, is, because he flies in daylight, too often killed for the crimes of his nocturnal cousin, the Great Horned Owl, but his food really consists of about eighty per cent mice.

However, it is impossible to generalize and say out-and-out that the Short Eared Owl doesn't do a lot of damage to game birds at times, since individual cases have been recorded showing extensive depredations among birds.

Among the owls which really do a job on rodents, but apparently only occasionally go after bigger prey, are the Barn Owl, Screech Owl, and Long Eared Owl.

Other owls, which on the whole do little damage to game birds, are the tiny "Saw Whet Owl," the very small Pygmy Owl, the Barred Owl, and the Burrowing Owl.

The snowy owl, not often seen in most of our states, sometimes comes down from the north when game is scarce, and, although of great beauty, is a known game bird and small animal predator.

DO BEARS BREATHE WHILE HIBERNATING?

BLACK BEAR

GRIZZLY BEAR

In the suspended condition of animation under which bears live while holed up for the winter, known as hibernation, the animals breathe, but not so deeply or fully as when completely animated.

Female black bears in the North produce young while hibernating—but, possibly due to slowed up physical processes, the young are very tiny and helpless.

A peculiar habit of bears in some localities just before they go into hibernation is to pick out marshy spots where their feet sink a foot or two in the mud and promenade back and forth for fifty to seventy-five yards!

Whether this is due to eliminating parasites, or a desire to get into condition, your guess is as good as ours!

DO YOU KNOW YOUR QUAIL?
Facts About America's Most Widely Hunted Native Bird

SKETCHES BY HARRY LIVINGSTON IN NATIONAL SPORTSMAN

BOB WHITE

GAMBEL'S QUAIL

SCALED QUAIL

MOUNTAIN QUAIL

CALIFORNIA "VALLEY QUAIL"

MEARNS QUAIL

BOBWHITE

Bobwhite, the common quail of the east, known for his beautifully musical "Bob White—Bob White" call, ranges throughout the temperate Atlantic slope and along the great Mississippi watershed. More American hunters are interested in quail shooting than in the pursuit of any other native game bird. The cock quail has black and white markings on the head, which distinguish him from the female, whose markings are buff and brown.

GAMBEL'S QUAIL

Gambel's Quail is a bird of the desert, and consequently, where cover is scarce and low, is often a runner and a skulker, for protection when hunted, rather than a seeker of safety in flight. Its range extends from southeastern California to Western Texas and south into Mexico.

SCALED QUAIL

Scaled Quail are also desert dwellers, and they can disappear as fast on foot, when pursued, as Gambel's Quail. Colorado, and the area south and west of that state, are its naural range. The peculiar, scale-like arrangement of the feathers is responsible for its name.

MOUNTAIN QUAIL

This handsome member of the quail family is shown here in only one drawing, since both the male and female are alike in plumage. It ranges over the Pacific slopes from Southern Washington to Central California.

CALIFORNIA "VALLEY QUAIL"

Crested like its cousin, Gambel's Quail, the California "Valley Quail" is confined in its natural range to California and slightly north and south of that state. However, it has been introduced successfully in other suitable areas. Although a fine game bird, it is often found close to towns and villages, and many times in them! The chicks are practically born running, as, when frightened, they will dash from the nest for cover with the shells still clinging to their backs!

MEARN'S QUAIL

Mearn's Quail is more plentiful in parts of Arizona and New Mexico than in other sections. In fact this particular quail is not at all widely distributed.

WHAT'S A MOUNTAIN BOOMER?

Why, it's a sewellel, a small, light brown animal of stubby build, living in only a few areas of California, Washington, and Oregon. It is about 12 inches long, with short ears, has a rudimentary or almost no tail, lives in burrows, and feeds mostly at night on vegetation. The natives call it both "Mountain Boomer" and "Mountain Beaver."

FIRST GAME LAWS WERE GREEK

Because the Athenians went hunting and didn't tend their mechanical duties, Solon forbade the killing of game.

HE'S GOT FEATHERS ON HIS SHINS!

Of all American game birds of the fowl type, grouse are the only ones with feathered forelegs. Every variety of grouse seems at first glance to be wearing leggings.

SPRUCE OR CANADA GROUSE

DUSKY GROUSE

SOOTY GROUSE

SHARP TAILED GROUSE

PRAIRIE CHICKEN

LESSER PRAIRIE CHICKEN

SAGE GROUSE

Grouse, while swift of wing and wary by instinct, and to most sportsmen one of our most difficult birds to shoot, seem to be on the wane in most parts of the country. In fact the Sage Grouse, once found in great numbers in the dry sagebrush country from British Columbia south to New Mexico, has become scarce despite its great range.

Even the "fool hen," "Canada," or "Spruce Grouse," as it is varyingly called, although still plentiful in many regions of northern New England and Canada, has greatly decreased from the vast flocks from which the Indians often took many moons of food supply in a single hunt.

Other famous grouse, certainly not increasing in numbers, are the Prairie Chicken, or Pinnated Grouse, of the Great Plains area northward to Manitoba, the Sooty, and the Dusky, Grouse of the Rockies, and the Lesser Prairie Chicken (smaller than the plains Chicken), of Oklahoma and Texas.

Grouse have far greater handicaps to contend with than being hunted. Although protected in many Plains and Rocky Mountain states, the settling and cultivation of the land seems to work them worse injury than booming shotguns.

As civilization advances, and brush and grass fires, together with close grazing by cattle and sheep, destroy grouse cover, these magnificent American game birds find increasing difficulties in rearing their families. All grouse are ground-nesters, and the chicks and eggs are both destroyed by fire sweeping through the grass and brush, and by clearing operations conducted by man, all of which also leave grouse without cover and protection from predators.

GROUSE PECULIARITIES

A Grouse chick is born with a little tooth on his bill, which he uses to chip himself out of the shell, and then sheds for good.

Foolhens, or Spruce Grouse, show signs of jealousy toward other females of the same species.

Spruce Grouse are all dark meat, while the ruffed grouse has white meat on the breast. "Sharptails" and Prairie Chickens also have dark meat on the breasts.

The Ptarmigan goes all his brother grouse one better —he not only has feather leggings but they extend well over his toes!

The Ptarmigan, mottled brown with black tail in summer, with white wings, turns all white in winter.

Efforts to introduce the Blackcock of Northern Europe to Maine, New York, and Canada have utterly failed. This great grouse has unique red feathers over its eyes, like eye-brows, and has a curly tail!

Some hunters have been so rash as to maintain that male ruffed grouse will not "drum," or make their booming love note (from beating the breast and wings) at night. However, many others have established the fact that occasionally this bird actually drums in the dark.